THE NEW IMMIGRANTS SERIES

Allyn & Bacon

Series Editor, Nancy Foner, State University of New York at Purchase

Contents

Foreword to the Series

The United States is now experiencing the largest wave of immigration in the country's history. The 1990s, it is predicted, will see more new immigrants enter the United States than in any decade in American history. New immigrants from Asia, Latin America, and the Caribbean are changing the American ethnic landscape.

Until recently, immigration was associated in the minds of many Americans with the massive influx of southern and eastern Europeans at the turn of the century. Since the late 1960s, America has again become a country of large-scale immigration, this time attracting newcomers from developing societies of the world. The number of foreign-born is at an all-time high: nearly 20 million foreign-born persons were counted in the 1990 census. Although immigrants are a smaller share of the nation's population than they were earlier in the century—8 percent in 1990 compared to about 15 percent in 1910—recent immigrants are having an especially dramatic impact because their geographic concentration is greater today. About half of all immigrants entering the United Sates during the 1980s moved to eight urban areas: Los Angeles, New York, Miami, Anaheim, Chicago, Washington, D.C., Houston, and San Francisco. America's major urban centers are, increasingly, immigrant cities with new ethnic mixes.

Who are the new immigrants? What are their lives like here? How are they redefining themselves and their cultures? And how are they contributing to a new and changing America? The *New Immigrants Series* provides a set of case studies that explores these themes among a variety of new immigrant groups. Each book in the series is written by a recognized expert who has done extensive in-depth ethnographic research on one of the immigrant groups. The groups represent a broad range of today's arrivals, coming from a variety of countries and cultures. The studies, based on research done in different parts of the country, cover a wide geographical range from New York to California.

Most of the books in the series are written by anthropologists. All draw on qualitative research that shows what it means to be an immigrant in America today. As part of each study, individual immigrants tell their stories, which will help give a sense of the experiences and problems of the newcomers. Through the case studies, a dynamic picture emerges of the way immigrants are carving out new lives for themselves at the same time as they are creating a new and more diverse America.

The ethnographic case study, long the anthropologist's trademark, provides a depth often lacking in research on immigrants in the United States. Moreover, many anthropologists, like a number of authors in the *New Immigrants Series*, have done research in the sending society as well as in the United States. Having field experience at both ends of the migration chain makes anthropologists particularly sensitive to the role of transnational ties that link immigrants to their home societies. With firsthand experience of immigrants in their home culture, anthropologists are also well-positioned to appreciate continuities as well as changes in the immigrant setting.

As the United States faces a growing backlash against immigration, and many Americans express ambivalence and sometimes hostility toward the latest arrivals, it becomes more important than ever to learn about the new immigrants and to hear their voices. The case studies in the *New Immigrants Series* will help readers understand the cultures and lives of the newest Americans and bring out the complex ways the newcomers are coming to terms with and creatively adapting to life in a new land.

NANCY FONER
Series Editor

Acknowledgments

Chinese immigration to the United States started 140 years ago. The old Chinese immigrants, however, differ greatly from the new arrivals. Although the adaptive patterns of the new immigrants have been of considerable interest, detailed ethnographic studies of the new immigrants are still in short supply. I was pleased that Allyn & Bacon, under the editorship of Nancy Foner and Sylvia Shepard, initiated this much needed series on immigration which includes the new Chinese. I would like to thank Nancy and Sylvia for their insightful comments and their editorial assistance. Both are wonderful people to work with and are professionals who are highly efficient, supportive, persevering, and productive. I am thankful also to my editorial assistant, Ms. Jennifer Green, who efficiently did the word processing, coding, and copy editing.

Finally, I wish to express my gratitude to the many members of the Chinese community in San Francisco who always have been willing to help me in my field research, in particular, to Ling-chi Wang, Him Mark Lai, Kenneth Quan, Margaret Wong, Wynnie Wong, Susanna Wang, Alex Leung and Bill Wong. Last but not least, I am grateful to the new Chinese immigrants who have assisted me in collecting life history materials and other relevant field data. Naturally, I am solely responsible for all lacunae and mistakes.

BERNARD WONG
San Francisco

Introduction

The Chinese population in the United States, according to the census of 1990, is 1,645,472. In 1960 it was 237,292. In a period of 30 years, the increase has been eight-fold. The most important factor accounting for the enormous growth has been immigration. Many of the Chinese are new immigrants who have arrived since 1965. The places which have attracted these new immigrants are major metropolitan areas, especially New York, Los Angeles and San Francisco. Ethnography on the new Chinese immigrants has been scant. Although there are now 315,345 Chinese in the San Francisco Bay Area (U.S. Census of 1990), and more than half are new immigrants, there has been little discussion of the adaptive patterns of the new Chinese immigrants in the Bay Area. By comparison to the New York area, which has 261,722 people of Chinese ancestry (U.S. Census of 1990), the San Francisco Bay Area has emerged as the largest population center for Chinese in the United States.

The new Chinese immigrants come from different social and economic backgrounds and possess different social and economic resources. The focus of this book is on how the new Chinese immigrants use their ethnic and personal resources to make economic adaptations in their new country. Instead of viewing the immigrants as victims of circumstances, I follow an actor-oriented approach, which sees them as problem solvers and decision makers who attempt to shape their own destinies.

Three sets of theories guide this work. The first deals with ethnic entrepreneurship (Waldinger 1989; Waldinger, Aldrich and Ward 1990; Wong 1987a, 1988; Light 1984; Greenfield, Strickon and Aubey 1979). As suggested by these authors, I will examine the opportunity structure available to Chinese immigrants in the U.S. Second are theories of adaptive activities and social transaction

(Barth 1966; Benedict 1979; Wong, McReynolds and Wong 1992). I will focus my attention on how Chinese immigrants use their non-economic resources such as family, kinship ties, community and cultural values to interact with the economic environment. Third is the set of theories that deals with the world economy, e.g., transnationalism and world systems theories (Wallerstein 1974, 1979; Basch, Schiller and Blanc 1994; Rosaldo 1993; Kearney 1991; Fong 1994). The enlargement of economic activities from narrowly confined spaces such as national states or regions into a wider geographical arena has affected many minorities, including the ethnic Chinese in the United States. Hence, it is necessary to examine how the world economy has influenced the social and economic life of the Chinese immigrants.

ETHNICITY AND ECONOMIC ADAPTATION

Ethnic culture is an important resource for the economic activities of the immigrants. In traditional social science literature, an immigrant's traditional culture was deemed to be baggage and a liability impeding economic mobility and full adaptation to American life. Recently, the tide has turned. Writers like Alejandro Portes (1990), Roger Waldinger, Howard Aldrich and Robin Ward (1990) and Ivan Light (1984) claim that ethnicity is a resource that is instrumental in many immigrant economic activities. The new Chinese immigrants use not only their ethnic resources, but also other personal resources such as education, special skills and social networks.

This book is about how the new Chinese immigrants use their ethnic resources (such as ethnic expertise, values, traditions, and social organization, the ethnic press, and access to ethnic consumers), class and economic resources (such as education, money, property, special knowledge) and personal resources (such as family connections and personal contacts) to respond creatively to the opportunity structure of the United States and the changing economy of the world (Fong 1994). Inevitably, this focus requires a look at the entrepreneurial activities of Chinese immigrants. As Chinese entrepreneurs interact with their economic environment they do not go blindly to just any job or any place to make a living. They have to assess what they can do and what is available; they have to make decisions about what comforts to give up and what talents or abilities to cultivate. Needless to say, these decisions are made within the context of the resource structure of the larger society.

The case of Mr. Chan illustrates these processes and also introduces themes about immigrant entrepreneurship and success that will come up in later chapters. (All the names used in this book are pseudonyms, except those belonging to public figures and well-known individuals in the community.) Mr. Chan was born in China but left in 1958 for Hong Kong, where he was able to get a job with Air France because he knew French. In the 1960s, Mr. Chan was hired to teach Chinese to the Chinese community of Madagascar, a job he held for about ten years. In 1970 he was sponsored by his sister in California to come to the United States, although he settled in New York's Chinatown. He got his first job as a bookkeeper for a business organization because he had earned a college degree in accounting in China many years before. Mrs. Chan got a job in a sewing factory.

With two wage earners, the Chans were able to support four children, ages five, seven, nine and eleven, and they rented a substandard two bedroom apartment. All four children went to a Chinatown public school and a day-care center every day while their parents worked. Mrs. Chan was determined to find a way to make a better life for her family in America. Originally a school teacher, she had also worked in a Chinese school in Madagascar, but she had never learned English formally. Knowing that in America the ability to speak English is crucial, Mrs. Chan enrolled in an evening English program. To save time in caring for her children she did major cooking three times a week—on Saturday, Sunday and one weekday—and then froze the foods for use the rest of the week. When the children came home from school, the oldest would warm the food for the rest of the children.

To maximize the family's income, Mr. Chan got a second job in a liquor store through an old friend in Chinatown. Since he did not drink and was a hard worker, his boss was very pleased with his performance. Mr. Chan continued to hold two jobs for a number of years. At the same time, he went to real estate school to get a realtor's license. Eventually he was able to quit his job as a bookkeeper and purchase a liquor store with family savings. In 1980, he sold the store and started a sewing supply company, which he thought would be a good investment given the proliferation of garment factories in Chinatown in the 1970s, and the lack of sewing suppliers in the area. In fact, Mr. Chan opened the only sewing supply store in New York's Chinatown. Business was brisk and soon he was able to open a second store, which his wife managed after quitting her factory sewing job. Mr. Chan hired kinsmen to staff his stores.

On the side, he also sold houses as an agent for a real estate company. This job gave him the opportunity to learn about the real estate world, knowledge he put to good use in speculations in the strong 1980s real estate market. He bought commercial property with friends at low prices and sold at high prices. Meanwhile, he kept both sewing supply stores running so he would have another business to fall back on in case the real estate market collapsed. In fact, Mr. Chan's foresight saved him when the real estate business was doing badly in the early 1990s. His two supply stores continue to do a brisk business, and in the past twenty years the Chans have been able to support all four children through college. One of the Chan daughters earned a Master's degree in accounting and is now running the main sewing supply store for her father. Mrs. Chan remains manager of the second store, assisted by relatives. The older son graduated from Yale Law School; the younger son graduated from Cornell with an engineering degree. Both daughters attended St. John University. Meanwhile, the Chans have purchased a large house in an exclusive area of Long Island with seven bedrooms, five bathrooms and a swimming pool. Theirs is truly a Cinderella story.

Recalling their arrival in New York's Chinatown, Mr. Chan told me that life was hard. The amount of savings the family had was small. They told themselves that they could only succeed, that they could not fail. They believed two things would help them solve their economic problems: hard work and good health. Mr. Chan chose work that he was trained for and Mrs. Chan did what she could do, sewing. Both of them learned from their jobs. They were keen observers of the economy and the demands of the opportunity structure whether in sewing supplies or real estate. Their success also had a lot to do with support from friends and family. Mr. Chan's sister gave some initial financial assistance to the family; his old friends in Chinatown got him his two early jobs, the bookkeeping position and the sales job at the liquor store. All of his partners in the real estate business were either old classmates or old friends from China.

When I asked Mr. Chan to tell me what led to his success in America, he explained:

Hard work and willing to put up with adversity is important. You have to understand what is needed in the economy and the opportunity available. One must have a vision. I was also fortunate to have my old friends in Chinatown who supported us. There was a saying in China that when you are at home, you depend on your family. When you are abroad, you depend on your friends. My friends got me jobs, loaned me money and gave me emotional support. My wife and my children assisted me all the way in the family business. They are the ones that you can trust. They also save me a lot of money. Trusted and inexpensive labor cost is very important to all Chinese ethnic businesses. I also came at the right time and the right place. The sewing supplies stores and the real estate business were in their peak in the 1980s when we started. We saw the opportunity and seized it.

I saw Mr. Chan again recently in San Francisco. He had been thinking of opening a garment factory supply store in San Francisco, but after much deliberation, decided against it because he has no other family members who can assist him in running the store. His two sons are now in law and computer science and are no longer interested in the family's enterprises. Mr. Chan felt that a supply store did not make sense when so many garment makers have moved their production plants to Third World countries. Finally, the overall economy has not been strong in recent years. Mr. Chan said that he is contemplating retirement in the next several years. He is grateful to this country, his community and his friends. Recently, he made a large cash contribution to a fund raising event which was designed to help needy children undergoing liver transplants in the San Francisco Bay Area. Mr. Chan is also active in the Chan Family Association. He is a financial backer of the association and supports its many worthwhile social projects, such as assisting immigrants to obtain employment and to locate schools for their children.

Not all new Chinese immigrants are as successful as Mr. Chan. Some have to toil without much financial return and with limited rewards. Others fail at business altogether. In general, however, the new Chinese immigrants are able to achieve economic independence, and very few are on welfare.

The new Chinese immigrants present an interesting case for study because they depend heavily on ethnic enterprises through which they create employment for themselves and others. Even many in professional fields want to set up their own businesses. Some come up against the glass ceiling in white establishments, feeling that they are not paid according to their capabilities and contributions. They perceive that as Chinese immigrant professionals they are handicapped in mainstream firms and they look forward to becoming their own bosses.

My exploration of how the different groups of Chinese use their ethnic, class, and personal resources in making a living and achieving economic success focuses on the San Francisco Bay Area. This is an area with varied economic opportunity where tourism, entertainment, garment manufacturing, high-tech industries, banking and insurance are the mainstays of the economy. Tourists come to San Francisco from around the world; Santa Clara, dubbed Silicon Valley, produces world-class computers and other high-tech products; and San Francisco, together with Los Angeles and New York City, is also an important fashion center in the United States. Chinese immigrants are attracted to the San Francisco region for a number of reasons. Not only does it border the Pacific Rim region; San Francisco has a moderate climate which is attractive to Chinese from Hong Kong, Taiwan and Southern China. San Francisco also has one of the oldest Chinese communities in North America. The region's economy offers opportunity for employment. Many are drawn to San Francisco because they have relatives and friends in the area. And, finally, San Francisco has many Chinese restaurants, grocery stores and Chinese-speaking residents, and thus offers a wide range of amenities and conveniences to the new Chinese immigrants.

The purpose of this book is manifold. First, it will show how the new Chinese immigrants have made their living in the San Francisco Bay Area. Second, in showing how they make a living and achieve economic success, the book tries to demonstrate the secret of ethnic entrepreneurship, which is a topic of great interest among social scientists (Waldinger 1989; Portes 1980; Light 1984). Third it aims to show how, in adapting to the American environment, Chinese immigrants have to make many sacrifices, both socially and economically. Through this book, I hope to dispel some of the stereotypes about immigrants in general and the Chinese new immigrants in particular. The new Chinese immigrants are not refuse from their homeland, as often depicted, nor are they a burden on the United States economy. They are not parasites of the larger society. Using their ingenuity, they have helped themselves and the larger society in a number of ways. Immigrants in general, and the new Chinese immigrants in particular, have made and continue to make tremendous contributions to American society.

The data on which this book is based have been obtained principally from fieldwork activities. Since 1986, I have collected data on the new Chinese immigrants by visiting their homes and their work places, participating in social activities and community functions, and observing the operation of grocery stores, Chinese restaurants, and garment factories. I have interviewed business managers, owners, and workers of Chinese business establishments both formally and informally. I have been involved and have worked in collaboration with community organizations. Some researchers complain that it is difficult to conduct fieldwork in the Chinese community because there are certain prerequisites to be met in working among the new immigrants. A researcher must have connections, such as through friendships, kinship and other networks, as well as the ability to speak the major Chinese dialects. I am fortunate in having both of these qualifications. As a member of an immigrant family with a large circle of relatives in the region, I have been able to gain inroads to the community. In addition, I speak both Cantonese and Mandarin, as well as a number of other dialects that enabled me to interview and communicate with the new immigrants from different regions of China. Kinship and friendship connections and dialect similarities create a certain warmth and ease in communication. Further, I have been able to add to the life history materials of my informants by keeping abreast of community activities, through participation and through the Chinese media.

In exploring the experiences of the new Chinese immigrants in the San Francisco Bay Area, I begin in Chapter 2 with a discussion of the history of Chinese immigration and the setting of this study. Chapter 3 looks at the reasons for the recent Chinese immigration; Chapter 4 considers the opportunity structures which are available to the Chinese and the various kinds of ethnic businesses such as Chinese restaurants, garment factories, and grocery stores. In Chapter 5 I examine how the Chinese use ethnic and personal resources to achieve economic success in their ethnic businesses. Chapter 6 demonstrates how the new Chinese immigrants use personal, cultural and class resources to function in the professional sector in the United States economy and to conduct international business around the world. It also addresses the role that the new Chinese immigrants play in the global economy. Finally, Chapter 7 looks at majority–minority relations and the ethnic identity of the Chinese.

From China to San Francisco

Southern China has been the principal source of both the old and new immigrants. Most come from the vicinity of the city of Guangzhou, in Guangdong Province. Stories of the immigrants, their failures and successes, get circulated in the home communities and encourage many come to America. The U.S. immigration law of 1965, which emphasized family reunification, has also favored the home communities of immigrants already in America. Many new immigrants initiated their first move from Guangdong through family connections in the United States.

The story of Meilee, a woman in her early forties, is a typical one for immigrants from mainland China. Meilee had been waiting since 1985 to get her immigration visa after she had been sponsored to come to the United States by an older brother in San Francisco. When her entry visa was finally approved in October of 1988 she immediately had to apply to her work unit in the city of Guangzhou for permission to leave China. Meilee was a graduate of a teaching training college and worked in an elementary school for many years. Her departure from the school had to be approved by her *Danwei* (work unit). She also had to be interviewed by the United States Consulate there. Her twenty-year-old daughter was allowed to travel with her, but her son was not because he was over the age of twenty-one. He had to stay behind in Guangzhou to continue to work, waiting for his mother to apply for an immigration visa for him once she arrived in the United States. The father, an architectural engineer, decided to wait with his son in China.

Thus both the father and son remained in China while mother and daughter made the trip to the United States, the Beautiful Country (*Mei Kuo*), to start a new life. What they had hoped for was not just a new economic life, but also a life of political freedom. Many new Chinese immigrants long to leave their total-itarian country, where families suffer from political purges and various political movements. Meilee and her husband were both considered "stinking intellectuals" and had been sentenced to hard labor during the Cultural Revolution. They had been accused of being counter-revolutionaries and were vilified because of their connections with the outside world—their rela-tives in the United States. During the Cultural Revolution, such connections earned people negative reputations, such as running dogs of the imper-ialists, spies, and counter-revolutionaries. Now that they were allowed to leave China, Meilee and her daughter were joyous because they no longer had to worry about such political instability and impositions. Yet Meilee and her daughter felt a great deal of sadness at having to leave behind half of their family. Departure became a sweet sorrow; they hoped that they would find a better life in America. They packed only minimally and departed for the United States via Hong Kong where Mei-lee's sister lived. Her sister loaned them money for their airplane tickets ($1,500 for two one-way tickets). Meilee and her daughter arrived in the United States in February of 1989 and they were met by relatives in San Francisco. After one week, both mother and daughter had found jobs: one as a temporary worker in a Chinese restaurant, the other in a garment factory.

Unlike the illiterate villagers of a previous era who came to work for mining companies or to build railroads, many new immigrants from mainland China, like Meilee, come to America with educational credentials and skills. The new immigrants often have kinship connections to the established ethnic commu-nity in the country. In fact, some immigrants have relatives who have been in the United States for many generations.

"Where Do You Come From?" "How Long Have You Been Here?" Chinese Americans are often asked these questions in the United States, the assumption being that the Chinese presence is new in this country. In fact, not all Chinese Americans are recent immigrants and their ancestors have been in this country for as long as the ancestors of many white ethnic groups.

THE HISTORY OF CHINESE IMMIGRATION

When did the Chinese first come to America? Some claim that they were here in the 4th century A.D., long before Christopher

Columbus (Fang 1980; Steiner 1979). Others claim that the Chinese arrived a thousand years ago (de Guignes 1761). However, according to reliable historical records, the first large influx of Chinese immigrants to the United States dates from the 1850s (Wong 1982). The number of immigrants steadily increased over the years, and peaked in 1890 with a population of 107,488. Discriminatory legislation, such as the Chinese Exclusion Act of 1882, the anti-Chinese Scott Act of 1888, and the Geary Act of 1892 were designed to prohibit the entry or reentry of Chinese immigrants who were laborers, thus putting an end to the influx of Chinese immigration. By 1920 there were only 61,639 Chinese in the country. Racism and fear of economic competition from the Chinese were the principal factors contributing to discriminatory legislation. It was not until after World War II that Chinese immigration recommenced, although significant influxes did not become apparent until the passage of 1965 immigration legislation.

Initially, in the 1850s, the Chinese settled on the West Coast, where they found jobs as railroad workers, miners, farmers and domestics. They have been a presence in the state of California ever since. Upon completion of the Central Pacific Railway in 1869 and the closing of many mining companies, Chinese and white laborers alike had to leave the railroads and mines to look for other forms of employment in California (Sandmeyer 1973; Wu 1958).

Economic competition with Whites led to various anti-Chinese campaigns in California and the passage of discriminatory legislation. One example was the Sidewalk Ordinance of 1870 which outlawed the Chinese pole method of peddling vegetables and carrying laundry in San Francisco. Traditionally, the Chinese carried heavy loads balanced on a pole which rested upon their shoulders. The pole functioned as a fulcrum. The Sidewalk Ordinance was directed specifically against the Chinese since non-Chinese people used wagons or carts to peddle their goods. There were ordinances against the use of firecrackers and Chinese ceremonial gongs, which were important symbols of luck and necessary implements for Chinese festivities. In 1871 the Cubic Air Ordinance was enacted in San Francisco, requiring each adult to have at least 500 cubic feet of living space. The law was specifically directed against the Chinese who were living in cramped quarters in extended family living situations. The Queue Ordinance, passed in 1873 in San Francisco, was another example of legislation specifically targeting Chinese. Under Manchu law, Chinese men were required to comb their hair into long braids, or pigtails, called queues. Cutting off their queues was a serious violation of Chinese law. After the passage of the Anti-Queue law, gangs of roughnecks began to attack Chinese people with long hair, cutting off their braids and wearing them as trophies on their belts and caps.

There were numerous laws prohibiting the Chinese from working in federal, state, county or city governments. The Chinese were barred from the fishing industry in California. There were laws prohibiting the education of Chinese children in the public schools in San Francisco and using Chinese people as witnesses against white defendants in court. Chinese were barred from purchasing property outside of Chinatown in San Francisco. In addition to these federal and state laws, in 1882 Congress passed the Chinese Exclusion Act, which prohibited Chinese laborers from entering the country (Wong 1982).

The Chinese responded to these legislative acts and discrimination by entering businesses such as Chinese restaurants and laundries which were not directly competitive with white enterprises. They organized self-help, community and protective societies. Many moved to the major metropolitan areas of the United States such as San Francisco, Los Angeles and New York City where they could attract a large clientele for their ethnic businesses. As a result of this movement, Chinese enclaves known as Chinatowns were developed. By 1940, there were twenty-eight Chinatowns in the United States (Lee 1947, 1960). From the 1880s to 1965, the Chinese depended almost entirely on ethnic businesses for their survival. In Chinatown they developed an ethnic economy which catered to both Chinese and non-Chinese customers. Their protective societies and associations were based on kinship, friendship, locality of origin, trade and dialect. Through these associations the Chinese mediated their own disputes, promoted their own economic interests and socialized among themselves. Although the establishment of Chinatowns proved to be a successful adaptive strategy, their creation was a direct result of racism. Discrimination, nonacceptance, and exclusion of the Chinese by the larger society compelled them to engage in limited economic activities within the confines of Chinatown.

As discrimination against the Chinese diminished and they became more accepted by the larger society, the Chinese were able to move out of the Chinatowns and to pursue other economic activities. By 1955, there were only sixteen Chinatowns in the United States (Lee 1960). With the influx of new immigrants after 1965, some Chinatowns expanded. The already existing Chinatowns of San Francisco, Los Angeles and New York all got a boost to their populations as new arrivals tended to move into preexisting Chinatowns. Chalsa M. Loo (1991) has noted that 81 percent of the Chinese living in San Francisco's Chinatown in 1990 were foreign-born. Among them were large numbers who had arrived after 1965.

Before 1965 the Chinese in the United States were a rather homogenous group in terms of their occupational, linguistic, social and economic backgrounds. Most of the Chinese immigrants came from the rural area of the Guangdong Province in southern China, particularly the Sze Yap and the Sam Yap districts. The lingua franca used in the Chinese community was the Taishan dialect. The kinds of structural principles used to organize the community were those common to rural China: kinship, locality of origin, regionalism, and dialect similarities. During the pre-1965 era, many immigrants were sojourners who had no intention of staying in America permanently. They reasoned that after they had made enough money in America they would return to China to become entrepreneurs or they would lead blissful lives of retirement. It was primarily economic factors which propelled Chinese immigration to America.

Initially, the Chinese worked mostly as laborers. After 1884 Chinese financial survival was entirely dependent on ethnic niche businesses such as Chinese restaurants, laundries, grocery stores and gift shops. In general, the early immigrants were less educated than post-1965 immigrants and mostly came from rural areas of southern China. They were predominantly men who had left their families in China. Various pre-1945 immigration laws had prevented the entry of Chinese women into the United States. After 1945 however, the War Bride Act and the G. I. Fiancees Act enabled Chinese women to enter the United States. Still, only Chinese G. I.s benefitted from these new legal provisions. As a result, in the pre-1965 era, the sex ratio between males and females was highly uneven, with males dramatically outnumbering females. The Chinese community was labeled a bachelor community. The lack of family life and children was a principal reason that juvenile delinquency was not a problem.

THE NEW AND OLD IMMIGRANTS: A CONTRAST

Since 1965 the Chinese community in the United States has changed dramatically. Of major importance was the enactment of the Immigration Act of 1965 which abolished national origins quotas and established a system of preferences whereby immediate relatives, skilled and unskilled workers, refugees, scientists, and technical personnel were listed under different categories of preference. For the first time Chinese immigrants were treated equally with other nationalities by United States immigration law, thus ending some eighty-five years of bias against the Chinese.

What has been the impact of the 1965 law on Chinese immigrants? First, any Chinese citizen who has certain family connections in America can be sponsored for migration by relatives in the United States. New immigrants can now come with their spouses and children who are under the age of twenty one. This scenario is significantly different from the one that existed in the past. In the nineteenth and early twentieth century most immigrants arrived individually as laborers, as their spouses were prohibited entry. After 1965 the new immigrants came with their families. Hence, the sex ratio between males and females evened out.

The new immigration law has also encouraged highly skilled immigrants trained in science, technology, the arts, and other professions. They applied for immigration visas under the Third Preference. At present, new Chinese immigrants are, as a group, relatively well-educated and many are from urban areas of China: Taiwan, Hong Kong or Macao. These immigrants differ significantly from earlier ones who came primarily from rural areas and were relatively uneducated.

In contrast to the early immigrants who mainly came from Guangdong Province, the new immigrants include larger numbers from different parts of China: Taiwan, Hong Kong, and other provinces of mainland China. However, Guangdong Province in mainland China is still the main source of new immigrants to the United States. Most of the new immigrants who are urban in origin use the standard Cantonese dialect of Hong Kong, or Mandarin, rather than the Taishan dialect used by the old immigrants in the past. Now, the Chinese television stations in San Francisco use both Cantonese and Mandarin. In the evenings, there is an hour-long Chinese News broadcast in Cantonese and another fifteen minutes in Mandarin.

While the old immigrants were mostly sojourners, the new immigrants are interested in making America their permanent home. The new immigrants' attitudes toward the United States are reflected in the phrase, *Lo Di Sheng Gen* (after reaching the land, grow roots). As soon as they are eligible, many apply for U.S. citizenship. In fact, 48 percent of the Chinese in the Bay Area are U.S. citizens. These immigrants wish to establish roots and commit themselves to their new country and they come relatively prepared to do so. The majority of the Chinese from Hong Kong belong to the middle class, and some arrive with significant savings or capital. Rather than leaving China to escape poverty, like the old immigrants, the recent immigration is, in large part, fueled by political instability. The new immigrants admire the freedom and democracy of the United States and they intend to establish their roots in this country.

Given their resources, many of the new immigrants have avoided the traditional paths to employment through ethnic businesses like restaurants, groceries or gift shops. Some own or are employed in garment factories. Some are employed in Caucasian establishments. Others have branched out to areas of manufacturing, transportation, construction, wholesaling, finance, insurance and agricultural services. Thus there is more diversity in the economic pursuits of the new immigrants as compared to their predecessors. Although there are economically disadvantaged immigrants, especially from mainland China, the traditional images of Chinese coolies and penniless immigrants do not apply to the majority of recent Chinese arrivals.

THE CHINESE IN THE SAN FRANCISCO BAY AREA

The San Francisco Bay Area has been home for Chinese immigrants for more than 140 years. This area contains the largest Chinese population in the country. In actuality, there are two Chinatowns in the San Francisco Bay Area. One is located in San Francisco and the other in Oakland. The Chinatown in San Francisco is the oldest and by far the most famous in the United States. The San Francisco Bay Area has been important for the Chinese for a number of reasons. First, its location on the Pacific Rim provides a convenient entry port as well as a mild climate, appealing to immigrants from a similar climate across the Pacific. Secondly, the Bay Area offers a wide diversity of employment opportunities ranging from jobs in the thriving ethnic economy to those in the high-tech and computer industries. This ready availability of jobs in different sectors of the economy attracts a diverse group of Chinese immigrants.

Consider a few examples. Mr. L came from Hong Kong with the intention of opening a restaurant in the Bay Area. In Hong Kong he had been the manager of a well known restaurant. As he told me, he did not have the training and good enough English to obtain lucrative employment in a white establishment. He saw his future in the ethnic niche, which he entered when he arrived. "To work with something that is familiar rather than not familiar" was his justification for going into the Chinese restaurant business in San Francisco. His first job was working as a waiter in a Chinese restaurant; two years later he opened up a small restaurant of his own. Another immigrant from Taiwan, told me that she liked the climate in San Francisco and the availability of employment in her field of biochemistry. She had been looking for jobs in the San Francisco Bay Area for quite some time. Finally, a position opened up in her field at a pharmaceutical company in the South Bay, and she has worked there since 1989. Another immigrant from Hong Kong first got a job working in the Midwest. After many years of job searching in the Bay Area, he finally found a position in a computer company in the Silicon Valley. He was pleased to have a job in the Bay Area because he said that this region has so much to offer to a Chinese immigrant.

For most immigrants, what is crucial is the existence of a long-standing Chinese community in the San Francisco Bay Area and a thriving ethnic economy. There is a large concentration of Chinese people, businesses and services that cater to Chinese consumers and provide convenience and a familiar culture. There are many Chinese restaurants, grocery stores, movie houses, schools, community, and professional organizations. Immigrants often have relatives in San Francisco who can help them find a place to live and a job. Along with informal support systems of kin and friends who have settled in the area, there are specific services designed to help newcomers. For example, San Francisco's Chinatown provides a manpower training center that is available to new immigrants who wish to become chefs, waiters, bartenders, seamstresses, and restaurant managers. Many Chinese immigrants first come to Chinatown, learn English and gain skills, and then move out to other localities within and outside of the Bay

Area. Apart from this, the Bay Area is host to a wide range of ethnic groups and is relatively tolerant of new immigrants.

RESIDENTIAL PATTERNS

The residential patterns of Chinese immigrants today are more complex than they used to be. In the old days, Chinatown was the place that Chinese lived in San Francisco. Today, the Chinese are scattered throughout the Bay Area. The city and county of San Francisco has, by far, the largest Chinese population among the five counties of the Bay Area. According to the 1990 census, the Chinese population in San Francisco itself was 127,140. Less than half live in Chinatown and its vicinity; the rest are distributed throughout different neighborhoods according to their social and economic status. In general, Chinatown houses most of the pre-1965 old immigrants and new immigrants from the People's Republic of China (PRC) who together constitute almost half of the immigrant population in the city.

San Francisco's Chinatown is the oldest and most important Chinatown the United States. Historians believe that the Chinese started settling in the area near present day Sacramento Street around 1848 to 1849. By 1850s, 789 Chinese were living in San Francisco (Chin, Him and Choy 1975; Kwang 1987; Davis 1929) and a year later there were thirty-three Chinese general stores, fifteen apothecaries, five restaurants, five butchers, five barbers, three tailors, three boarding house, three wood yards, two bakers and five herb doctors in the Sacramento and Dupont area, known then as Little Canton or Little China (Kwang 1987) Beginning in 1850 Chinese district associations were created to serve the immigrants. By 1869, The Chinese Six Companies: (now known as the Chinese Consolidated Benevolent Association) was organized (Hoy 1942). Throughout the years, prejudice and laws that forced the Chinese to live in Chinatown structured the growth of ethnic businesses, while at the same time creating a segregated community.

After World War II, restrictive ordinances in San Francisco were lifted due to the China-U.S. wartime alliance. Chinatown still maintained its strong ethnic identity, but Chinese movement to other neighborhoods began.

Significant changes in the residential patterns of the Chinese came about more completely after 1965. With the influx of new immigrants from Hong Kong and China, more Chinese moved into the Richmond district which is about a dozen miles west of the old Chinatown. Often called the New Chinatown, this area has a population of 30,000 and boasts many Hong Kong restaurants and stores catering to the new immigrants. In fact, 50 percent of homeowners in the Richmond district are Chinese. In the past ten years, concentrations of Chinese stores and Chinese residents developed in the Sunset district, south of the Richmond district. In these new areas, there are many Chinese restaurants, specializing in Chinese regional cuisines, as well as Chinese supermarkets, video shops, hair salons, bakeries, book shops, and grocery stores. The ethnic economy of the Chinese has moved beyond the boundaries of the Old Chinatown on Grant Avenue. Today more than half of the city's Chinese residents in San Francisco no longer live in downtown Chinatown. Many have moved out of San Francisco altogether, into Santa Clara, San Mateo, Contra Costa and Alameda counties. In fact, of the approximately 320,000 Chinese in the Bay Area about 60 percent live outside of San Francisco. Nevertheless, San Francisco's Chinatown remains a capital and symbolic center for all the Chinese in the Bay area.

CHINATOWN: THE SYMBOLIC AND CULTURAL CENTER

San Francisco's Chinatown is a neighborhood, a work place, a social center and a community which helps immigrants adjust to a new land. As an entry port for newcomers to the New World, it is continually replenished with the traditional culture of the homeland. Newly arrived immigrants to the community get their first experiences with the United States there and learn how to obtain employment, a social security card, and open a bank account, to speak English and understand their rights and obligations as members of American society. San Francisco's Chinatown is, in short, an acculturation agent for the new immigrants. The community has bilingual social service agencies, translation services, Chinese stores, familiar food supplies, Chinese mass media, and information networks, all of which cater to the needs of the new immigrants. Newcomers can visit traditional herbal medicine stores, temples and churches, which provide tremendous security to new Chinese immigrants, especially those who do not speak English.

San Francisco's Chinatown is also a symbolic center of Chinese culture in the United States. Entering from the main entrance of Grant Avenue, one immediately sees a Chinese style gate which has an inscription from Dr. Sun Yat-sen: "All under heaven is for the good of people." The golden characters, which are inscribed on a blue plaque, may simply seem exotic to tourist, but to recent Chinese immigrants they offer consolation and comfort. Chinese immigrants are proud that Chinese culture exists in America. Seeing the sign for the first time, the newcomers feel that there are other Chinese who live and work here. As they see storefronts carrying Chinese signs, they tell themselves that "I don't have to be afraid, I can manage here; I know where to shop and to get around."

Chinatown is a convenient place for immigrants who do not speak English. They can find employment in the ethnic enterprises in the enclave and shop in many of the Chinese grocery stores. Food and Chinese produce are relatively cheap in Chinatown due to the concentration of restaurants and grocery stores which compete with each other. The immigrants who speak only Cantonese also find Chinatown a safe haven where they do not have to deal with unfamiliar language and customs. People are addressed by kinship terms, and human interaction seems to follow the Old World pattern. Almost all of the stores in Chinatown have Chinese employees who speak the language of the new immigrants. There are Chinese bookstores, Chinese newspapers, and recreational centers catering to the new immigrants.

The Richmond and Sunset districts are well connected to Chinatown through the downtown area by the city's transit system. The Chinese residents of the two districts often do their shopping in Chinatown. Some wealthy Chinese immigrants choose not to live in any Chinese neighborhoods but prefer exclusive areas like St. Francis Wood, Sea Cliff, Nob Hill and the Marina. These new immigrants consider their expensive homes to be their best long term investment and believe that houses in good neighborhoods will appreciate in value.

Many middle class immigrant Chinese also live outside of the new or old Chinatowns in places like San Mateo, Burlingame, Millbrae, and Foster City which are situated in the south of the city of San Francisco and belong to the county of San Mateo. The 1990 census indicated that 32,487 Chinese lived in San Mateo county where there are now a number of Hong Kong style restaurants, shops, and grocery stores. Chinese people who live in San Mateo tend to speak English and drive automobiles. Many who work in San Francisco have to drive to work, about a 15–30 minute trip to reach San Francisco. San Mateo has a wealthy neighborhood called Hillsborough where the average home is sold for one million dollars. The very affluent new immigrants prefer to live in Hillsborough where the climate is moderate throughout the year, the schools are said to be good and many first class Chinese restaurants are close by. Both the international airport and the city itself are within comfortable driving distance. Hong Kong businessmen who sell their expensive homes in Hong Kong can afford to live in this area.

Santa Clara County in the south of San Francisco is home to another 65,027 Chinese (U.S. Census 1990). As Chinese immigrants move up economically, they tend to move northward geographically, starting from San Jose and ending in the Palo Alto/ Menlo Park areas. Most of the Chinese who live in Santa Clara are connected with engineering, computer, and high-tech businesses. Some are professionals working in banking, accounting, insurance, law and financial establishments. They are the professionals or technical people: many have Ph.Ds or other advanced degrees.

In San Francisco's East Bay, in Alameda county, there are 68,585 Chinese according to the 1990 census. Many new Chinese immigrants live in the Chinatown area of Oakland. The Chinatown there is much smaller than San Francisco and has fewer Chinese restaurants and stores. The affluent Chinese immigrants in the East Bay prefer living in the Oakland Hills and Piedmont areas. These are desirable neighborhoods because houses are bigger and have more amenities and the schools are said to be better, too. Some Chinese also live in Berkeley. In Contra Costa County the 22,106 Chinese immigrants live in the cities of Concord, Richmond, El Cerrito, Hercules, San Ramon, Orinda, Lafayette and Walnut Creek. In general, the farther away from San Francisco, the cheaper the houses are. Although many new immigrants in Contra Costa County are middle class, others work at menial jobs in places like Chinese restaurants. Finally, Marin County in the North Bay is an expensive bedroom community for people who work in San Francisco and is home to Chinese professionals and business people who work in San Francisco. They speak English, drive automobiles and are comfortable living in a white suburban environment.

CHINESE ASSOCIATIONS

Chinatown's associational structure was organized according to principles which are familiar to the immigrants. There are regional and district hometown associations as well as trade, kinship, and dialect associations. There are also modern associations such as alumni associations, labor union, social agencies, and political parties.

Traditional Chinese associations in San Francisco at one time numbered more than a hundred, and formed themselves into an associational structure. At the top of this structure is the Consolidated Chinese Benevolent Association, known as the Chinese Six Companies. The associations played an important role in the past. Composed of Chinese from the six major district associations—the Ning Yung, Kong Chow, Young Wo, Shiu Hing, Hop Wo, and Yan Wo—the Six Companies served as spokesmen and official representatives for the Chinese in San Francisco. Before the establishment of the Chinese Chamber of Commerce in 1910, the Six Companies also regulated Chinese business activities, mediating business disputes and arbitrating conflicts between various family and district associations. The Six Companies arranged the shipment of bones of deceased immigrants back to China for re-burial. They also issued clearance for immigrants to return to China, making sure that all returnees first paid their debts in America. The Chinese Six Companies ran the General Chinese Hospital and Chinese schools; they also organized the celebration of the Chinese New Year and various fund raising activities for the community. Although many of their functions are no longer needed, the Chinese Six Companies remain the highest authority, at least symbolically, of the community.

The Chinese Six Companies adopted an anti-Communist stance and were strong supporters of Nationalist China. This is perhaps because the Chinese Six Companies are controlled by the older Chinese who either suffered under Communism or embraced an anti-Communist ideology. In the past, the Six Companies assisted the Kuomintang in their overthrow of the Manchurian government in China.

In recent years the Chinese Six Companies have come under attack from radical students and community workers for being too slow to adapt and meet the needs of the new immigrants. What these critics often overlook, however, is that most of the traditional associations and in particular the Chinese Six Companies were established before 1965 to serve the needs of adult, male Chinese old-time immigrants and they are not prepared to tackle contemporary social problems such as housing, Medicare, and ju-venile delinquency (Wong 1979).

The various family or clan associations in San Francisco's Chinatown recruit members on the basis of common surname. The largest family associations are the Lee, Chan and Wong associations. Within the family name associations are the *fongs* which group people according to both common surname and common village or origin. In China, the family name or surname group was an exogamous (or out-marrying) group, and members addressed each other as clan brothers (Tien 1953; Wong 1979). The surname group was thus a clan group whose members were assumed to have descended from a common ancestor. In China, the fongs were localized lineage groups and membership was based on patrilineal descent (through men in the male line) from a common ancestor associated with a village.

Family name associations have assumed important functions in San Francisco. Many family name associations here maintain temporary lodging quarters for their members. These common lodging rooms are called "common Fong." Thus the word Fong has two meanings. One refers to common kinship origin in China, the other to the living quarters in the family name associations. What is significant is that kinship has been used as a principle of social organization to address the needs and problems of the Chinese community. Within the family name associations, there were once informal credit clubs called *hui* that operated on a voluntary basis. Members of the club made contributions to a fund that was given to a person who needed the money and was willing to pay back the amount each member put in along with interest. The way a hui worked was that a number of people, ten for instance, would agree to contribute $1,000 to form a total pool of $10,000. The member entering the highest bid (i.e., who bid to pay back the amount with the highest interest) would get the entire amount of $10,000. In return, he had to pay $1,000 to each member plus interest. After repayment to all of the members, say in ten months, the hui would be dissolved. This kind of informal credit arrangement is no longer practiced by the family name associations for it is rather risky and is not enforceable by law. Credit unions and banks are now the institutions new immigrants use for loans. One association, the Lee Family Association, has its own credit union for members.

In San Francisco there are now some multifamily name associations. One of the most important is the Four Brothers Association, which was organized by the Liu, Kwan, Chang and Chao families because their forebears swore brotherhood by the Peace Garden Oath two thousand years ago for the purpose of saving the Han Dynasty. Another multifamily name association is the G. How Oak Tin Association which is composed of the Chan, Hu, Yuan, and Wang families, all of whom claim descent from the Shun Emperor. The Chee Tuck Sam Tuck Association is composed of the Wu, Tsai, and Chow families who were once neighbors in China. Similarly, the historical friendships among neighbors in China have led to other associations. Loui, Fong, and Kwong families united to form the Soo Yuen Association; the Gon, Lai and Ho families became the Sam Yick Association. Perhaps the most interesting of all is the Chew Lun Association, which united the Tam, Tan, Hsu and Hsieh families based on a similarity (a common radical) in the Chinese characters used to spell their names.

In single family name as well as multifamily associations, kinship ideology has been deliberately embraced, and kinship terms are used by members to address one another. The family name associations still exist today, attracting mostly older immigrants; they provide recreational facilities such as reading rooms and mahjong tables, perform limited welfare services, and organize scholarship funds and ancestor worship.

Regional associations, which are composed of members from a certain county or region in China are another level of organization. Like family associations, they are basically mutual aid societies rendering welfare and employment assistance; the larger associations generally offer temporary lodging facilities. Some even provide aid for burial service. The Vietnam Chinese Association has an informal insurance company which collects fees from members to form a fund to help families pay for funeral services.

Business and trade associations form another cluster of associations in the social structure of Chinatown. The Chinese Art Goods Association, Chinese Chamber of Commerce, Chinese Apparel Contractors Association, Chinese Laundry Association, and Golden Gate Neighborhood Grocers' Association are some examples. These associations often negotiate with the larger society on matters of concern to Chinese businesses. As information centers, they channel information and regulations on taxes, sanitation, wages, licenses, and legislation. For example, the Chinese Chamber of Commerce recently voiced communitywide concern about the removal of Highway 480, asking the city government to help organize the traffic flow through Chinatown and set up parking facilities for customers of Chinatown businesses.

Another group of associations called Tongs have their roots in China as secret societies which fought against the Manchu government. In the past, the Tongs in Chinatown were involved in illegal activities such as prostitution, gambling and opium smoking. The Tongs have now dissociated themselves from their criminal past and today many call themselves merchant associations. Suey Sing Merchant Association, Yee Ying Merchant Association and Ying On Association are some examples of Tongs.

The traditional Chinese associations I have mentioned now mainly serve social and recreational functions. Some offer scholarships to students and maintain a place for ancestral tablets. Some even have cemeteries. In fact, these associations tend to be particularly significant for the Chinese who have leadership capabilities or aspirations but are unable to become involved in civic or social organizations in the larger society due to a lack of English fluency. Many well-to-do Chinese donate money for scholarships and charity work and look to leadership positions in the traditional associations as a way to gain recognition and prestige. However, new immigrants from Hong Kong and Taiwan who speak English and live outside the confines of Chinatown generally have little or no interest in joining the traditional Chinese associations.

Modern associations such as alumni associations, political parties, and social agencies have become more important for the Chinese community than the traditional associations. Now organizations such as the Chinese American Citizens Alliance, Chinese for Affirmative Action, Chinese Newcomers Service Center, Chinatown Youth Center, Chinatown Neighborhood Improvement Resource Center and On Lok Health Services for the elderly play a significant role in the lives of the new immigrants.

Chinese businessmen are drawn to modern business associations such as the Chinese Merchant Association and the Chinese Chamber of Commerce, both headed by Chinese women with political connections to City Hall and the larger society. The modern business associations lobby City Hall and local politicians for the improvement of neighborhood safety, parking facilities, and on issues concerning construction of highways which can affect Chinese businesses in Chinatown.

CHINATOWN AS A CENTER OF ETHNIC RESOURCES

San Francisco's Chinatown is a social, economic, and recreational center for the ethnic Chinese in the San Francisco Bay Area and in many ways, it has come to also symbolize Chinese political power in city politics. Chinatown has several Chinese movie houses, Chinese newspaper publishers, hundreds of ethnic restaurants, Chinese book stores, and Chinese language schools. It houses the largest Chinese General Hospital outside of Asia as well as a home for the aged. Interestingly, San Francisco's Chinatown is more connected socially and politically to the larger society than other Chinatowns in the United States, including the one in New York. Officials of the Chinese Chamber of Commerce and neighborhood associations have considerable influence in San Francisco's City Hall. Non-Chinese elected officials of the city frequently tour Chinatown especially during election periods. Some elected Chinese officials hold special office hours in Chinatown. Many of San Francisco's Chinatown new associations and social service agencies are influential outside as well as within the community. These include the Chinese For Affirmative Action Inc, Newcomer Social Services and the Chinatown Resource Center. The annual Chinese New Year Parade—the largest Chinese New Year parade outside of China—is attended by more than one million people; many of the viewers and participants are not Chinese and people come from far away as China and Japan to witness and participate in the event.

San Francisco's Chinatown is a well-known icon and has been featured in American mass media, from movies to music to television to newspapers and magazines. It is an important tourist attraction for both domestic and international tourists. It is also home to many Chinese, and a place that has a special resonance for many other Chinese who do not live there. Representatives of Bay Area political organizations, schools, universities, media, and business are all involved in the Chinese New Year celebration. The two prominent corporate sponsors are the Bank of America and the San Francisco Chronicle. The parade boasts numerous floats, lion dancing troupes, and a fifty-meter dragon controlled by more than a hundred athletes. Downtown traffic is completely rerouted to accommodate the festivities. Many radio stations and two local television stations have continuing coverage of the festivities from about 6 P.M. to 10 P.M. in the evening. The parade culminates with a fire display and firecrackers exploding in the air.

As the symbolic heart of San Francisco's Chinese community, Chinatown continues to exert a pull for American-born Chinese who now live elsewhere. Many come back to visit to renew cultural ties, attend social functions, to shop and help the community. Some of these second-generation Chinese-Americans have helped to organize ethnic interest associations to promote Chinese civil rights and the fair distribution of resources from the larger society.

Chinatown is more than the noise of firecrackers, the aroma of incense from temples, the taste of Chinese food, and exotic shops, and glittering gold characters. These are the material artifacts that tourists come to see and experience. For Chinese immigrants, Chinatown is a real community: a place to live; a neighborhood which offers psychological security, jobs and job training, and information about America; and a place to socialize with each other in their own language and according to Chinese etiquette. Through their organizations, the Chinese find emotional, economic and social support in Chinatown. Any Chinese can find a group to join there. For instance, Mr. Wang, a new immigrant from China has the option to join the multifamily name association G. H. Oak Tin, the regional association of Chin Lien, or the language association of Hakka. In any one of these groups, he would be able to meet and socialize with individuals who share his own Chinese name, home region, and dialect and develop networks that may well help him find employment.

San Francisco's Chinatown is, in fact, a manpower training and employment center for immigrants, especially those who do not speak English. Many chefs, seamstresses, and Chinese restaurant managers are trained in San Francisco's Chinatown. It serves as a springboard to a new life in a new land. After having tested the waters in San Francisco's Chinatown, many Chinese immigrants move to other communities in the Bay Area and throughout the United States.

Take the case of Ms. Chu. Migrating from mainland China in 1989 where she obtained her high school education, Ms. Chu got her first job working as a Dim Sum waitress in a Chinese restaurant in San Francisco's Chinatown. There co-workers told her about the Chinatown Resource Development Center. After three months of basic training in word processing and data entry at this nonprofit manpower training center, Ms. Chu got a job in a Chinese bank as a part-time data entry clerk. Advised by her Chinatown career counselor at the Center that to succeed in America she had to learn English and go to college, Ms. Chu enrolled at San Francisco's City College (a two-year community college) where she took English and general education courses for three years while continuing to work part-time at the bank. In 1993 Ms. Chu was accepted at a four-year college to study computer science. After receiving her B. A. degree, she got a raise in salary and a full-time job at her bank. Today, Ms. Chu holds a better, higher-paying position at a different bank in the South Bay. From Chinatown and the Chinese bank, she has moved to an affluent suburb and a larger white-owned bank. Ms. Chu is now fluent in English and moves at ease within mainstream American society. Ms. Chu is just one of the many examples of how immigrants receive initial support and training in Chinatown and then move on. For many new immigrants, Chinatown works in this way as a stepping stone into the larger society.

At the same time, Chinatown is a center of cultural continuity. The community observes a Chinese calendar and celebrates seasonal festivals with various specialty shops in Chinatown selling items needed for the particular occasions. On weekends and during Chinese holidays, hundreds of Chinese immigrants celebrate various ethnic festivals in Chinatown. In addition to the annual Chinese New Year Parade, on the fifth day of the fifth month of the Chinese calendar, the community celebrates the Dragon Boat Festival. All of the Chinese restaurants in Chinatown offer special food, glutinous rice wrapped in bamboo or lotus leaves; grocery stores in the community carry the ingredients so people can prepare special food for the occasion at home. On the fifteenth day of the eighth month of the Chinese calendar there is the Mid-Autumn Moon Festival where Chinatown bakers make moon cakes for their customers. There is also a Winter festival observed more by the new Chinese immigrants than the old. Sweeping-the-Grave festivals occur in the spring and autumn when the Chinese visit the graves of loved ones. In addition to these major festivals, some Chinese in the community celebrate the Beggars' festival on the seventh day of the seventh month of the Chinese calendar. On the ninth day of the ninth month of the lunar calendar, children fly kites. Many American-born Chinese have forgotten some of these festivals, but the new immigrants tend to celebrate a number of them. For the children of immigrants, the festivals provide an important link to Chinese culture; they often develop fond memories of Chinese culture through these ethnic events.

Because it is customary for the Chinese to have elaborate funerals for their loved ones, funeral processions are common in Chinatown. A hearse, led by a white convertible carrying a portrait of the deceased, is accompanied by a marching band and followed by a motorcade. Effigies and monies are thrown into the streets by mourners for use by the deceased. After the funeral, surviving family members host a dinner in Chinatown for all of the mourners. Similarly, it is customary to have a party for newborn babies at their one month birthday where the family may host a dinner in a Chinese restaurant. Chinatown's restaurants are also used for wedding banquets and other celebrations. In all these ways, Chinatown is a place for immigrants and others to practice traditional customs and maintain a sense of Chinese culture.

Who Are The New Chinese Immigrants?

Many Americans unfamiliar with the history of the United States and the new Chinese immigration movement still think of immigrants as the refuse of their societies. A common belief is that immigrants cannot make it in their own societies and come to America in search of the American Dream. Some still think that immigrants are here for religious freedom, like the Puritans and Pilgrims of the past.

Many of these outmoded popular beliefs must be modified and corrected with data that have been obtained on the new Chinese immigrants. While it is true that many immigrants in the past came to America solely for economic betterment, this is no longer so for many of the latest arrivals. In the case of the new Chinese immigrants, motivation for immigration is complex and requires viewing it in a larger context which involves global, national, community as well as individual personal factors. The latest immigration of Chinese into the U.S. has been shaped by social and economic conditions in China, immigration laws, political factors in the sending and receiving countries (Portes and Rumbaut 1990; Zhou 1992), social conditions in preexisting immigrant communities as well as global economic factors and personal circumstances facing the Chinese.

THE SOURCES OF THE NEW CHINESE IMMIGRATION

In the nineteenth century, Chinese emigration was widespread especially from the coastal regions of Fujian and Guangdong. At that time, most Chinese migrated to the Pacific Islands, Latin America, and the United States. Traditionally, the South Seas was a favorite destination for the Fujianese, Tiochiew and the Hakka (Amyot 1973; Tien 1953; Wong 1979). Most of the Chinese from the Sze Yap and Sam Yap districts of Guangdong province came to the United States (Lee 1960; Wong 1979). Today Chinese immigrants comprise a much more diverse group, from three principal sources: mainland China, Hong Kong and Taiwan. Immigration from each of these areas is limited by quotas imposed by the United States. The People's Republic of China has a quota of 20,000 immigrants per year, while Taiwan has a separate quota of 20,000 (Mangiafico 1988). Hong Kong, as a colony of Great Britain, used to have a colonial quota of 600 slots per year. In 1985 the United States increased the quota for Hong Kong natives to 4,364 per year; residents of Hong Kong who were born in China are included in the quota for mainland China. Because immediate relatives of United States citizens are not limited by these quotas, the United States now allows the legal admission of about 40,000 Chinese people a year (Mangiafico 1988).

The three groups of immigrants also differ in their exposure to capitalism and entrepreneurship. Hong Kong and Taiwan immigrants tend to be more westernized than Chinese mainlanders. The first two groups are more familiar with the American economic and political system, whereas mainlanders tend to overestimate the affluence and opportunities available in the United States. Religious freedom has not been a significant factor in the immigration of either the Hong Kong or Taiwan Chinese immigrants, as both of these nations enjoy relative freedom of religion.

Reasons for immigrating to the United States vary depending on the countries of origin. Economic factors are not the key ones for those coming from Hong Kong and Taiwan. In fact, in the past three decades Hong Kong and Taiwan have thrived economically as a result of the shift of manufacturing centers from industrial countries to Asia. Living standards have improved and a relatively large middle-class has developed. The Chinese from Hong Kong and Taiwan have migrated to the United States principally for the education of their children and long-term political stability that their home countries do not have.

Economic and political factors are the two major causes of the large movement from mainland China. Although mainland

China has achieved considerable growth in recent years, many Chinese have not directly benefited from the economic gains, especially those in rural areas and those who lack political connections. Some have lost hope in communism and socialism and long for political freedom. The majority of mainland Chinese immigrants look to America to improve their economic lot and to enjoy personal freedom. Thus while economic considerations play an important role in the migration of mainlanders, many immigrants from Hong Kong and Taiwan leave a better economic situation at home to find political stability and educational opportunities in the United States.

The preexisting Chinese communities in the United States also play a role in the immigration decisions of the latest Chinese arrivals. Families and kinsmen in the United States often encourage their relatives to come to join them. In fact, nearly all Chinese immigrants obtain visas on the basis of the family reunification provisions of U.S. immigration law. Some Chinese businesses in Chinatown also need help. The shortage of labor has prompted many to invite their relatives to work in their labor-intensive family businesses where trusted workers are sought who can contribute their labor as well as assist the family head in supervising major tasks. Thus, for instance, Andrew Lam, who had three garment supplies stores, sponsored his brother to come to help him. Andrew had two stores in New York City and one in California. The two stores in New York were run by himself and his wife. In California he needed a manager. His brother was able to join him in 1989 and became the manager of the California store.

Some immigrants have come to America for personal reasons. After the Tiananmen incident in 1989, many students and scholars from China decided to apply for political asylum because of their personal involvement in the Chinese Democracy Movement. Harry Wu's case exemplifies the personal factors in this kind of immigration. Born in 1937 in China, Harry Wu was arrested as a rightist in 1960 for his criticisms of the 1956 Soviet invasion of Hungary. He spent nineteen years in a Chinese prison. The *San Francisco Chronicle* (May 19, 1996) reported that after his release, Harry Wu came to the United States in 1985 and has been devoting his life to expose the darkside of China's penal system. He became a U.S. citizen in 1994 and sees himself as a champion for human rights in China.

MAINLAND CHINA: IMMIGRATION ENTHUSIASM

Since 1979 the People's Republic of China has relaxed its exit requirements, prompting many Chinese mainlanders to consider migrating overseas. Permission to leave China to join one's family is generally granted if a person can prove that he or she has obtained a visa from a receiving country. Short-term visas are granted to students to study overseas and to officials and business organizations for conducting business abroad. Applications for exit visas from China have been abundant.

There are many reasons for the current exodus from mainland China. Some cite the repressive political situation and restrictive economic system. Some believe that social mobility is too constrained by factors related to political connections and family background. It is a common belief that if one is not a member of the Communist Party or a child of a high ranking government official, one may not be able to move ahead. Many mainlanders have grown weary of the constant political movements and upheavals in China. The political situation is indeed peculiar: an individual might be considered a national hero one day and accused as a counter revolutionary the next. Among those seeking to leave China are intellectuals who have suffered personally from the various political and social movements and reforms. Some intellectuals have been interned in labor camps or sent to villages for incorrect thought or for not following the timely ideologies of the appropriate political leaders.

Although China has achieved some economic success in recent years, people living in rural areas still suffer from grinding poverty and deprivation. Some peasants in Fujian province have to work extremely hard just to feed their families. They make less than $30 a month at the same time as there has been high inflation. Prices for food, clothing, and other daily necessities have increased much faster than wages. Believing that there is no chance to have a good life in China, many rural Chinese long to migrate to America, which has been portrayed as the land of opportunity. Lured by glowing reports of the United States and its wealth, thousands of Chinese peasants save money to pay individuals to smuggle them to the United States. Some pay smugglers a portion of the total cost and promise to pay the balance with wages from future employment in America. Smugglers may charge $30,000 to $40,000 per person to take people to the United States (*San Francisco Chronicle*, April 29, 1993). Despite these costs, not all potential immigrants reach their destinations. In 1994 there was extensive media coverage in the United States of the arrests of thousands of illegal Chinese immigrants trying to reach California and New York.

The preexisting Chinese communities in the United States serve as a motivating factor for immigrants from China who have heard of the success stories of their compatriots in various American Chinatowns. Some are confident that they can easily find employment, even without speaking English, in New York or San Francisco Chinatowns. Rumors have it that ethnic businesses such as Chinese restaurants, garment factories, and grocery stores, always need Chinese workers. Although tales about the good life in America are exaggerated, a good number of immigrants do have relatives in this country who can help and facilitate their initial settlement. Some Chinese business owners in America do need workers and hence sponsor their relatives from China. Thus, the preexisting Chinese communities in America are like magnets attracting the immigrants from the motherland.

THE UNCERTAIN FUTURE OF HONG KONG: 1997 AND BEYOND

Hong Kong was originally a fishing village. The island was seceded to Britain after China's defeat in the 1840 Opium War. The British also acquired a 100-year lease on the territories north of Hong Kong. Today, Hong Kong is a bustling and vibrant place with a robust free enterprise system. It has generated much wealth for Great Britain and has created a large middle class among the Chinese. Located in the southern part of China about 80 miles south of the city of Guangzhou, Hong Kong is a transportation, financial, manufacturing, and trade center of Asia. It has a harbor which is visited by thousands of sea-going vessels. Products manufactured locally can be shipped to any location in the world, and products from overseas can be transported and unloaded in Hong Kong for subsequent transfer to locations throughout China. Hong Kong serves as an important link with the global economy and as a link between China and the West. The five million people inhabiting Hong Kong constitute a relatively cheap labor resource for garment manufacturing, electronics, and the construction trades. Many refugees from China are willing to work hard for low wages in Hong Kong; Hong Kong's economy underwent tremendous expansion after the 1949 Communist takeover of China. In the past 40 years, the Hong Kong economy has grown rapidly as a result of low taxation, cheap labor, and high productivity.

Many immigrants reluctantly have left Hong Kong for two principal reasons. One is to have their children educated in the United States and the other is the political uncertainty of Hong Kong. The city has only two major universities which can admit only 800 students per year, from a population of 5 million. As it is, many families who can afford it send their children overseas for university education. As for political factors, many of the inhabitants in Hong Kong are former refugees and have personally suffered from communism in China and dread the prospect of having a communist regime in Hong Kong. On the one hand, they are proud of the fact that the Chinese people can reclaim their territories from Britain. On the other hand, they worry about the loss of personal freedom and the free enterprise system after the city's return to China.

According to an agreement between Great Britain and China, Hong Kong and its contiguous territories must be returned to China in 1997. As of this writing, it is unclear whether Hong Kong will continue to have a free enterprise system under communist rule for an extended period of time. Although Deng Xiaoping pledged that the current economic system of Hong Kong will continue for another fifty years, many Hong Kong residents are skeptical. Many believe that there is no future for their children and families in Hong Kong.

The residents of Hong Kong are too familiar with the politics of the Chinese Communist Party, especially those who have come from China. Even native born Hong Kong residents have friends or relatives in China and have first hand information about politics in China. They are familiar with the constant political upheaval, from the land reform movement to Rectification movement, and from the Cultural Revolution to the Tiananmen incident, and they are disturbed by the fact that many innocent people were wrongfully persecuted during these campaigns.

Fearing the worst, some Hong Kong Chinese have left for the United States, Canada, Australia, New Zealand and the United Kingdom, all politically stable, democratic countries with free enterprise and good university systems. It has been very difficult for the Chinese to move to the United Kingdom, stringent rules based on racial factors and birth place in British commonwealth disqualify many Hong Kong Chinese. Some Chinese have used investment visa quotas to migrate to Canada and Australia. Chinese with $175,000 to invest may qualify for investment visas in Canada. In 1990 the United States Congress also approved the issuance of investment visas; people who could invest from one to three million dollars in the United States were eligible for a visa of this type. This exorbitant amount has proved to be prohibitive to many Chinese investors. As a result, Chinese immigrants with only moderate investment capital have tended to emigrate to Canada or Australia.

TAIWAN: IS THERE A FUTURE?

Economically, Taiwan has been quite successful. Yet many natives of Taiwan prefer to send their children to the United States to receive education. They also want to have a secure home in a politically stable country like the United State or Canada. Like Hong Kong, Taiwan is another site undergoing dispute. The People's Republic of China has always claimed that there is only one China and that Taiwan, a province, is a part of it. As early as the seventeenth century, Chinese from the coastal region came to settle in Taiwan. The province was under the control of Japan for about fifty years, until the end of World War II when Taiwan became the twenty-second province of China. In 1949, Chiang Kai-shek and his followers were driven out of China by the Chinese communists. Since 1949 the Kuomintang (Nationalist Party) has ruled Taiwan while at the same time claiming to represent China. Under the Kuomintang, Taiwan has emerged as an economic power in Asia. Further, the Chinese in Taiwan have achieved affluence as a result of the economic restructuring of the world: many of the world's products are now assembled or produced in Taiwan. Both the domestic economy and foreign trade have grown tremendously, and the living standard is one of the highest in Asia, comparable to that of the United States and other industrial nations.

In addition to the disputed claims of legitimacy by the Chinese Communist party and the Kuomintang, there are periodic skirmishes between Taiwan and China on diplomatic fronts. The latest crisis concerned Taiwan's presidential elections of March 1996. Fearing that Taiwan may become an independent nation after the election of President Lee Ten-hui, the Chinese have started amassing military forces. Some people in Taiwan are worried about the eruption of military and political conflicts between the two regimes, concerned that China might invade Taiwan. With China's increasing insistence on reuniting Taiwan with the mainland, many Taiwanese are anxious over their future and are seeking places to migrate. Vancouver and San Francisco are favorite destinations due to the mild climates and geographical proximity to Asia.

An interesting transnational trend is that some immigrants, after migrating to the United States and obtaining a passport or green card, have returned to Taiwan or Hong Kong. They left their children and families behind and return to their homelands to continue their economic activities. Others, after first living in the United States, have gone to Africa, Latin and Central America to operate the business enterprises such as garment factories, restaurants and grocery stores. However, these immigrants are ready to return to the United States on a moment's notice.

The period of the late 1960s to the early 1990s has seen drastic global changes. Most important has been the transformation of the world economy. Industrial countries have shifted from predominantly manufacturing to service-based economies (Fong 1994; Sassen-Koob 1988), and manufacturing centers of the world have moved to low-cost areas such as Asia, Central America and South America. Beginning in the late 1960s and fueled by the Vietnam War, Asia has become an important center for the production of consumer goods for both the European and North American market, leading to an economic boom which encompassed Hong Kong and Taiwan. The newly settled Chinese from Taiwan and Hong Kong began sending their children to universities at home or overseas, leading to a relatively large population of highly educated Chinese. Many of these students have been educated in the United States and Europe and they are familiar with Western lifestyles, and have acquired a cosmopolitan outlook on the world. Yet these students also realize the fragility of their good life and the limits of Asian growth, especially due to the political uncertainties of the region. Many of these educated Chinese applied for immigration visas to work in the United States. How-ever, their education also allowed them to see the limit of growth in the United States. Some started to travel back to Asia or other parts of the world to look for better economic opportunity.

EDUCATIONAL AND OCCUPATIONAL BACKGROUNDS OF THE NEW IMMIGRANTS

Contrary to popular perception, the new Chinese immigrants are generally well-educated and a good number held important positions in their countries of origin.

Among the Chinese immigrants admitted to the United States during the period of 1982 to 1986, 15.8 percent held executive and managerial positions in China and 25 percent were in the professions. In terms of educational backgrounds, most new Chinese immigrants are better educated than the average United States citizen. According to 1990 census figures, Chinese immigrants have more high school and university graduates in their ranks than does the general American public. Their educational and occupational backgrounds may partially explain their economic success. In addition, the median household income for these immigrants is higher than the United States average. The popular image of immigrants as welfare recipients draining social funds is simply not applicable in the case of the Chinese.

The Chinese immigrants come from a tradition that values education, and with the surge of economic growth in Taiwan and Hong Kong, large sums of money have been allocated recently to the educational systems. According to the 1980 census, 80 percent of Hong Kong immigrants and 89 percent from Taiwan had a high school education, in contrast to 67 percent of the general U.S. population. Even immigrants from mainland China, with an average of 60 percent high school graduates, came close to the United States figures (Zhou 1992). Although it is relatively difficult for Chinese to go to universities in their home countries, among the immigrants there are proportionally more university-educated individuals than in the general homeland population. Within the United States, 1980 census figures show that while only 16 percent of the general population had completed 4 years of college, 30 percent of immigrants from China, 43 percent from Hong Kong and 60 percent from Taiwan had done so (Zhou 1992). In all the major counties in the San Francisco Bay Area, 1990 census data reveal that there are more Chinese with a B. A. or graduate degree than the U.S. average. Thus, for instance, in Santa Clara County, 1990 census data indicate that 20 percent of the Chinese immigrants from China, 28 percent from Hong Kong, and 38 percent from Taiwan have degrees from graduate schools as compared to the 7 percent of the general U.S. population. In other counties of the San Francisco Bay area, similar patterns exist.

Of course, the educational systems in Taiwan, Hong Kong and China are not comparable to each other or to the American system. In mainland China, the educational emphasis is on science and technology. Very few universities grant M. A. or Ph.D. degrees and the teaching is conducted in Chinese only. Some academic subjects are taught in an entirely different manner than in the United States. Thus, for instance, a Chinese can complete medical school in five years immediately after high school. Another example is that architecture and civil engineering often are taught together, culminating in an architectural engineering degree. Similarly, in Taiwan there is an emphasis on science and technology which attracts the best students. The less qualified study agriculture or enroll in law school. However, the quality of education in Taiwan is comparable to that of the United States and similar teaching materials are used. In Hong Kong, the universities are even closer to American and British universities. English is used as a medium for teaching, and textbooks and the quality of university faculty qualities are like those in Europe and the United States. Although some immigrants living in the United States do not work in their field of specialty, they nevertheless have intellectual tools which are helpful in solving problems and adapting to American life.

Immigrants who were educated in China may have problems with the English language when they arrive. There is also the difficulty of transferring their experience and skills to positions in the United States. However, after a brief period of downward mobility, many of the highly educated immigrants quickly learn English and find employment comparable with the jobs they had prior to emigration. Still, it is not uncommon to find individuals in positions in the United States very different from those they held at home. For instance, a former professor may open and operate a take-out restaurant. For those who have a serious problem learning English opportunities are especially limited.

Mr. Eng was an architectural engineer in China whose degree was not recognized in the United States. He thus had a hard time gaining employment in his field. When he first came to the United States, he started to work in a Chinese restaurant, giving him time to settle in and accumulate savings. Washing dishes and waiting tables was a job that he never dreamed of having in mainland China, but he had to do this to survive in the United States. When he worked in the restaurant, he got to know many construction workers and landscapers. He told them that he had an architectural degree from China. With some of these customers, he started to organize a business firm specializing in designing Chinese gardens and Chinese restaurants for other immigrants. Finally he had become his own boss and was doing work which matched his training.

ECONOMIC RESOURCES OF THE NEW IMMIGRANTS

Unlike earlier Chinese immigrants, many now come to America with substantial amounts of money. Many have had the opportunity to accumulate savings before leaving for the United States. This is particularly the case for Chinese citizens from Hong Kong and Taiwan, countries that have reaped the benefits of the shift of manufacturing from other countries to their home territories. Before coming to America many new immigrants also sold off businesses and properties, often worth a lot of money in Hong Kong. It is common for many new immigrants to come to the United States with significant amounts of capital, often as much as $150,000. Also many wealthy businessmen have transferred capital to the United States from Hong Kong and Taiwan in expectation of changes to come in 1997.

Take the case of one middle class Hong Kong family who came to the United States in 1988. Like many middle-class Hong Kong immigrants who came at this time, they ran a medium-sized restaurant and owned a condominium in Hong Kong, both of which they sold. Thus they were able to come to the United States with $200,000 in savings. The Chous used some of this money as a down payment to purchase a small condominium in San Francisco. Meanwhile, the husband and wife both worked in a Chinese restaurant to learn the ins and outs of running a business in America. In 1990 they bought a small fast food restaurant in the South Bay, converting it to a take-out Chinese restaurant with five tables for in-house dining. According to the Chous, this was a very difficult period during which both wife and husband worked from 7:00 A.M. to 10:30 P.M. every day. But their hard work reaped rewards: two years ago the Chous sold their restaurant to a buyer for $120,000, double the original $60,000 they had paid just two years earlier. As Mrs. Chou said of the sale: "The price is right!" From there the Chous planned to open a bigger and better restaurant.

Though fewer in number, there are also wealthy Hong Kong Chinese who have come to San Francisco. Mr. Gee and his wife were both successful business people in Hong Kong. Trained as architects, they ran a contracting company and a trading and an investment firm in Hong Kong. The Gees sent their son to study in the United States in the 1970s. After he received his Ph.D. in engineering, the son adjusted his visa to become a permanent resident and founded an engineering firm. Through their son, Mr. and Mrs. Gee got green cards and eventually both became legal residents of the United States. They returned to Hong Kong to continue their businesses there and channeled a good portion of their capital to the United States. With this, in 1989 the Gees built a number of multifamily homes in San Francisco's Sunset District, close to Chinese shopping areas. These homes sold quickly. Recently, the Gees have become involved in purchasing larger shopping centers with other Chinese investment partners from Hong Kong.

New Chinese immigrants thus often come with resources—financial capital, training, and education—that were unheard of among their predecessors a century ago. In addition, the opportunity to immigrate as a family, which did not exist for Chinese immigrants in the past, is a resource in itself. Family members can provide emotional support, and the family becomes an economic resource, providing a kin network for capital and manpower. Clearly, changing economic and social environments in both the sending and receiving countries affect the adaptations of new immigrants.

Economic Challenges and Responses for the New Immigrants

The new immigrants, whether they are rich or poor or from China, Hong Kong, or Taiwan, all experience uprooting upon their arrival. Many of the amenities and familiar people and life styles are gone. Some experience downward social mobility. Some have to change their jobs or their affluent life style. However, after an initial period of hardship, many Chinese new immigrants adjust to the new land. The overall economic performance of the new Chinese immigrants in the United States as compared to other ethnic groups is impressive. Not only are the household incomes of the new Chinese immigrants on average higher than the incomes of most United States households, but the number of new Chinese immigrant families living below the poverty line is smaller than for many other immigrant groups such as Hispanic, Vietnamese, Pacific Islanders, and Korean.

In the five counties of the San Francisco Bay Area, there are more than 18,000 Chinese-owned firms (*Asian Week* 1991). In San Francisco county alone, there are 9,028 Chinese firms drawn from a Chinese population of 127,140. This number amounts to approximately one Chinese firm per 14 Chinese persons. Most of these firms are family-owned and family-run ethnic businesses. In fact, Chinese immigrants depend on family ethnic enterprises and their education and training for survival in the United States. The Chinese enclave economy not only generates employment for the Chinese immigrants, but also, through business and invidividual income taxes, generates revenue for the city, county, state, and federal governments of the United States. Ethnic enterprises have been crucial for the new Chinese immigrants in their quest for economic independence and success. Even those who were relatively well-educated and held high school or college degrees in their homeland have trouble finding work outside of the ethnic niche if they do not speak English.

One adaptive strategy of the new immigrants is the exploitation of the ethnic niche established by their forebears. This includes the enclave businesses composed of Chinese restaurants, garment factories, gift shops, and other Chinatown-related stores. Of course, not all Chinese immigrants work in the ethnic economy. For the highly educated Chinese immigrants, opportunities exist outside it. There are, for example, jobs in businesses that work to develop goods for the mainland Chinese market. Also, the rapid growth in high technology ("high-tech") industries has created a demand for skilled labor. Since many Chinese are highly trained in technical and scientific fields, they are ideally suited for high tech jobs. Finally, some new immigrants have become involved in international import and export businesses.

ECONOMIC OPPORTUNITY FOR THE NEW IMMIGRANTS

In trying to understand how immigrants have become incorporated into the American economy some social scientists, like Michael Piore (1986) have emphasized that low-skilled and poorly educated immigrants move to the secondary sectors of the economy where employment tends to be temporary and unstable, wages are low, working conditions are poor and there are few opportunities for promotion. Piore suggests that as these jobs are abandoned by native workers who take better jobs in the primary sector (large corporations, unionized industries, skilled trades, government agencies, high technology industry, and the professions), secondary sector jobs become available to immigrant populations.

This may be the route for some immigrant groups, but most Chinese have been absorbed instead into the Chinese ethnic economy. The Chinese ethnic economy, which has expanded enormously in recent years, offers secondary sector jobs to co-ethnics in Chinese owned firms. Ethnic economies as many scholars observe, have their own dynamic, separate yet parallel to the core economy of the larger society (Portes 1980, Wilson and Portes 1980, Zhou 1992, Wong 1987a). In the small-scale enterprises that comprise the ethnic sector, common destiny, common language and cultural similarities are particularly important.

For the Chinese, the traditional ethnic economy, in place for more than 100 years in America, has been composed of Chinese restaurants, laundries, grocery stores, and gift shops. While these ethnic enterprises are still thriving today, changing demographics among the Chinese and a changing United States and global economy have also led to changes in the ethnic economy.

THE ETHNIC NICHE OF THE CHINESE

The economic behavior of members of an encapsulated ethnic group needs to be viewed in the context of its relationship to the larger society. It is within the macro–economic environment—the opportunity structure of the larger society—that the economic adaptations of an ethnic group are made. The macro–economic structures affecting the Chinese include environmental/market demand (Waldinger 1990; Wong 1987a) as well as government and immigration policies.

The Chinese did not come from a nation of laundrymen or restauranteurs. Nor did they start these businesses immediately after they first arrived in the 1850s. Occupational specialties are the result of their adaptation to economic and social conditions they encountered in the United States. The Chinese who came to America in the nineteenth century were principally laborers engaged in railroad building, exploitation of mines and clearance of farm lands in the western frontier. Along the transcontinental railroad and the western frontier, some Chinese restaurants were established, not as gourmet, luxurious enterprises, but as simple eateries to serve the Chinese laborers. Hand laundry shops were also established because there were no housewives or women to do this chore; since laundry was considered to be women's work, very few white men entered this trade.

From these frontier days, the Chinese learned that laundry was a low capital business with no competition from white people. With a little soap, some scrubbing boards, irons and ironing boards, a person could start his own business. The hand laundry business captured the attention of other Chinese who were discriminated against in the job market after the completion of the transcontinental railroad in the 1870s. Restaurants and laundry businesses have been important ethnic enterprises for the Chinese ever since.

The economic niche carved out for the Chinese has continued to develop throughout the 140 years of their existence in America.

In addition to restaurants and laundries, Chinese have opened garment factories, novelty and handicraft shops, and grocery stores in a number of urban areas. Until recently the Chinese had limited opportunities available in other fields. Many states had discriminatory legislation against the employment of Chinese. In New York State alone, there were 26 occupations which the Chinese were prohibited from entering, including such positions as: attorneys, physicians, bank directors, chauffeurs, dentists, embalmers, veterinarians, guides, liquor store owners, pawnbrokers, pilots, plumbers, horse track employees, watchmen, architects, CPAs, engineers, realtors, registered nurses, and teachers, among others. This legislation was not changed until as recently as 1940. There is also a long history of more subtle discrimination in employment and promotion. Moreover, many jobs need special skills, higher education and a good command of the English language, traits which disqualify many new immigrants and refugees without an American style education.

It was through ethnic businesses that the Chinese have been able historically to avoid economic conflicts with the larger society. As mentioned earlier, economic competition precipitated much of the anti-Chinese legislation in American history. Going into an ethnic business as a self-employed laundrymen or working in a Chinese restaurant were noncompetitive or nonconfrontational adaptive strategies, a way of avoiding persecution. Thus the continuation of the ethnic niche is a historical vestige and, in a sense, is a monument to racial discrimination.

The 1965 Immigration Law, which permitted the influx of Chinese immigrants, affected the development of the Chinese ethnic niche in terms of: (1) the availability of manpower, (2) the establishment of family firms, (3) the availability of capital resources, and (4) the infusion of urban entrepreneurs from Hong Kong, Taiwan, and China.

Many new immigrants, especially those from Hong Kong and Taiwan, arrived with skills and financial capital, as I have already discussed. Family members also provide important labor resources as well as sources of financing. These entrepreneurial assets have been instrumental in creating many changes in the Chinese business establishments. Because family members became readily available, many firms were now organized and run by family members. The majority of new immigrant entrepreneurs still prefer to run family firms that provide them with flexibility, independence, and control over workers. Decisions can be made quickly without lengthy consultation and the head of the family is also the head of the family firm. Family members can be trained in business operations; they are trustworthy and able to keep trade secrets; and they are willing to work long hours. Kinsmen of the family also constitute an inexpensive labor pool. And family members are an important source of financing. Many firms have been established through the pooling of family members' savings. In present-day Chinatown, almost everyone dreams of owning a family firm. It is not uncommon for firms that were started by a group of partners to split up sooner or later, with each individual moving on to try to establish his or her own business.

Originally, the majority of Chinese ethnic business in the United States catered to nonethnic consumers. Ethnic businesses still rely heavily on nonethnic customers and would not be able to survive without this clientele. However, since 1965 the Chinese community in the Bay Area has grown so much that there is now a substantial ethnic consumer market. In order to accommodate the recent influx of Chinese immigrants, many of whom have more economic resources than those in the earlier waves, the ethnic economy has expanded in the service industry in areas such as real estate, banking, and utilities. The wave of real estate purchases by Chinese in the 1980s created a market for Chinese real estate financing companies, brokers, contractors and construction workers. One can witness daily the construction and remodeling activities in the Asian populated Sunset and Richmond Districts in San Francisco.

Chinese Restaurants

The influx of immigrants from different parts of China has played an important role in the increase and diversification of the Chinese restaurant trade in America since 1965. At the same time, there has been a growing market for Chinese restaurants in the general population, probably because the restaurants are usually inexpensive, and Chinese food is tasty, fresh and generally non-fattening. The Chinese responded to the increased demand by (1) starting more restaurants, (2) enlarging the range of food served and adding Chinese cuisine from different regions of China, (3) renovating restaurants to emphasize Chinese ethnicity, for example, by adding Chinese decor and symbols, and (4) adjusting to the tastes of the American public.

As the Chinese immigrant population has expanded and diversified, so management styles have also changed as the popularity of Chinese food has grown in the United States and worldwide. Today, some Chinese restaurants are owned by regional and international chains, though most are still locally owned.

According to my informants in the business, there are probably more than 40,000 Chinese restaurants in the United States, employing more than 500,000 restaurant workers. These restaurants are concentrated in New York, San Francisco, and Los Angeles. Chinese restaurants are represented in practically every American city. There is also a new phenomenon as Chinese restaurants have moved into other ethnic neighborhoods, suburbs, and small towns. Chinese restaurant operators cater to customers who are not familiar with Chinese culture or Chinese food. Through the sale of Chinese food, they are often marketing Chinese ethnicity. In this regard, Chinese restaurants are actually outposts of Chinese culture. Many Chinese restaurants play Chinese music, feature Chinese costumes, serve Chinese beer, wine and other liquors, serve Chinese desserts, and celebrate major Chinese festivals with special foods. Lion dances and martial arts demonstrations are featured during the Chinese New Year. Eating out is not just a culinary event: it becomes an ethnic and cultural event. Some Chinese restaurant operators further specialize in take-out food, catering to office workers and suburban or small town dwellers.

Chinese restaurants have been able to meet the changing demands of their American clientele. For instance, when Americans began to show a preference for spicy dishes, Chinese restaurants responded immediately by inventing new hot sauces. When America turned to lower-fat, lower-sodium and non-MSG diets, Chinese restaurants responded by substituting vegetable cooking oil, increasing vegetarian dishes and avoiding the use of MSG (especially in suburban restaurants).

Experts estimate that as of 1996 in the San Francisco Bay Area, there are about 1,500 Chinese restaurants; the total number of Chinese engaged in the restaurant business there is about 15,000. Many of the restaurant workers are new immigrants from China and Hong Kong. Relatively few restaurant workers are from Taiwan as Bay Area restaurants have been dominated by the Cantonese. There are many varieties of Cantonese restaurants: some are Hong Kong style, others include Hakka, Tiochiew, and

Hainan cuisines. Additionally, there are other regional cuisines such as Hunan, Shanghai, Beijing and Szechuan restaurants. Most recently Thai-Chinese, Singapore-Chinese, Burmese-Chinese, Vietnamese-Chinese and Chinese vegetarian restaurants have come on the scene. Because of a demand for northern Chinese cuisines, many chefs from Hunan, Taiwan and Szechuan have been recruited, but the majority of the clientele in the Bay Area still prefer Hong Kong style Chinese cuisine.

The Chinese restaurants also have met the demand of their clientele through internal renovations and reorganization. This ability and willingness to renovate indicates the entrepreneurial character of the Chinese restaurateurs. Thus, for instance, the Hong Kong Flower Lounge in Millbrae has spent more than a quarter of a million dollars to create an Oriental atmosphere with a four-faced Buddha statue erected on a balcony to attract customers. Some owners have invented new menus for different occasions. There are also new methods of presenting food and serving customers.

Investment costs for a Chinese restaurant vary depending on size and location. A small take-out Chinese restaurant in the San Francisco Bay area may need a $60,000 to $120,000 initial capital outlay. A medium-sized restaurant will require about $200,000 to $300,000. Restaurants with a seating capacity of 300 may require a lot more. Many small- and medium-sized restaurants are family owned and family controlled. Because a family cannot manage a restaurant with a staff of less than twenty-five, some medium-sized or larger restaurants are run by groups of kinsmen or friends who are also shareholders. Very large restaurants are often run by local or transnational corporations because they may require millions of dollars of investment capital.

Some Chinese in the San Francisco Bay Area have established chain restaurants, such as Tong King, Harbor Village, Hing Lung, Hong Kong Flower Lounge, Yet Wah and May Lee's. Harbor Village has branches in Los Angeles, San Francisco, Toronto, Hong Kong and Kowloon. May Lee is a take-out restaurant with branches in San Anselmo, Fairfax, Mill Valley, and Novato. These restaurant chains tend to be owned by partners or business organizations.

In the Chinese restaurant business, working hours are long, as many as twelve hours a day, sometimes six or seven days per week. In many family-run restaurants, the working hours are even longer, especially for the owners and chefs who may well work fourteen-hour days, seven days per week. The gross salary per worker ranges from $1,500-$3,000 (including tips) per month for full-time workers. The story of Mrs. Lei illustrates the hard work involved in running a restaurant.

Mrs. Lei and Her Take-Out Restaurant. Mrs. Lei and her husband came to the United States in 1992. They tried a variety of jobs, but nothing worked out for them. In 1994 the couple purchased a restaurant for $40,000 in a small Bay Area town. After six months, some basic repair and improvement to the establishment was needed. Mrs. Lei went back to Hong Kong, where she was able to raise the needed $20,000 from her relatives and friends. Both husband and wife worked diligently to maintain the restaurant, rising early each morning to begin preparations at 7:00 A.M. and opening for business at 11:00 A.M. The restaurant had just four tables and seated only twelve people. Income came mainly from take-out and delivery. Peak business hours were from 11:00 A.M. to 3:00 P.M. and from 5:00 P.M. to 10:00 P.M. The only slow period, from 3:00 P.M. to 5:00 P.M., was a time of rest for the Leis: during this time they were able to go to the bank to make deposits and conduct other business. Every night they returned to their home after 10:00 P.M., only to wake up again at 6:00 A.M. Recently, a Chinese family made a very attractive offer to purchase the restaurant and the Leis sold for $100,000. Now the Leis are considering purchasing a medium-sized restaurant and involving more kinsmen to work in it.

In many cases, the family will learn the restaurant trade by working in restaurants, and then open their own when they can save enough money. For the Lee family, it was their son Johnny who provided the impetus to purchase a restaurant.

Lee Family Restaurant. Johnny came to the United States with his parents in 1969 and subsequently attended college here. During his college years, Johnny worked in Chinese restaurants part time. His parents also obtained menial jobs working in Chinese restaurants in Chinatown. As Johnny was the only son, it was expected that he would support his family. Yet Johnny realized that his work in restaurants would never be sufficient to improve his family's economic condition. After much discussion, planning and investigation, Johnny and his family decided to open a small Chinese restaurant themselves. As Johnny was the only person in his family with a college education and good English language skills, it was decided that he would become the manager of the family business. Johnny's father and mother both worked in the kitchen of their family-owned restaurant, joined by another relative working as the assistant chef. Various white American college students were hired to work as waiters/waitresses and delivery persons.

The restaurant started as a diner but is now a full-fledged restaurant with a seating capacity of fifty. From its inception in 1974, the restaurant has continued to be a family run, controlled and owned business. Johnny's family continues to work very hard. Both Johnny's parents start work at 8:30 A.M., beginning their day by chopping vegetables and doing the other preparation work that is needed for the lunch and dinner hours, and they do not return home until after 10:30 P.M. Johnny starts his day a little later than his parents, beginning at 10:30 A.M., but twelve- to fourteen-hour days are not uncommon for him.

These efforts have brought Johnny and his family many rewards. Johnny's parents and uncle own a house, as does Johnny and his family. Two of Johnny's children are enrolled in colleges. The family has several cars and can afford to take vacations periodically. Their life is similar to the life of the average American middle class family. Johnny confided to me in this way: "Having a business of your own beats working for someone. Although you have to work as hard in your own restaurant, you gain better economic results!"

Due to the lack of other opportunities, many new immigrants use the Chinese restaurant business to achieve economic success. They also use the restaurants to support the education of their children and to help their children find a place in American society. Unlike Johnny Lee, most of the children of immigrant restaurant owners are not interested in continuing in the restaurant industry. The second generation, after receiving college or specialized degrees, tend to look for work in the white establishments of the larger society. One restaurant owner told me: "The Chinese restaurant work is hard work. We are in it because we don't have other alternatives. We work like cows and horses. All that we do is for our family and our children. I hope that after they have finished their education, they do not have to be like us working in a Chinese restaurant like cows and horses." In short, the Chinese restaurant business is a survival strategy for the new immigrants.

In some Chinese restaurants, owners do not need to work themselves but hire other Chinese to work for them. Those tend to be highly profitable, large-sized Chinese restaurants. Not only are Chinese restaurants a source of profit and income for a large number of restaurant owners and restaurant workers, they also have a positive effect on the overall economy of the Chinese in San Francisco. Grocery stores, poultry farms, and vegetable farms in the Bay Area all profit from the continuous demands of the Chinese restaurants. So do fishermen, trucking companies, construction companies, and interior decorators. These are the multiplier effects of the Chinese restaurants on the local economy.

There are, however, some common problems facing both the owners and workers in Chinese restaurants in the Bay Area. One is the labor-intensive nature of the business. Not only do employees have to work excessively long hours, but owners also often have to work as hard as their workers. Another problem is the proliferation of Chinese restaurants competing for a finite number of customers, resulting in lower profit margins. To compensate, restaurants are forced to stay open for longer hours and to lower their prices. Many observers agree that the Chinese food sold in San Francisco is cheaper than in any other city in the United States.

Restaurants employ further tactics to increase profits, for instance, asking customers to pay in cash so that they do not have to pay commission to credit card companies. Tips from customers are divided among all of the restaurant workers as well as with management. In the past, most Chinese restaurants would provide free food to workers, but recently some restaurant owners have begun charging for food. Some consider this practice a form of exploitation; others consider it necessary because of the low profit margin of the business.

The Garment Factories

The development of the Chinese garment factory is directly related to the revised immigration policy of 1965, because only then were Chinese women immigrating to the United States in number, making seamstresses available. The majority of the Chinese garment factories are run by new immigrants.

Garment factories are highly competitive and their work is seasonal. The 500 garment factories in New York's Chinatown employ more than 20,000 Chinese workers in 1995. In San Francisco, I would estimate that there are 350 Chinese garment factories with a work force of 15,000 laborers. San Francisco is the third most important fashion center in the country, behind New York and Los Angeles. Most of the large garment manufacturers in San Francisco, like Levi Strauss and California Byer, use a subcontracting system, whereby materials are distributed to garment factories to be assembled. These subcontractors are typically Chinese.

Traditionally, Chinese immigrants in San Francisco, women in particular, worked in the garment industry in factories owned by nonethnics. However, over the past twenty years, many white owners have closed their factories in the United States, and moved their plants overseas to take advantage of cheap, foreign labor. The Chinese have seized this opportunity to acquire the old factories, reopen them and staff them with Chinese immigrants. In contrast to the turn-of-the-century Chinese immigrant community, comprised predominantly of men, the recent wave of new immigrants includes a large proportion of women, many of whom learn to sew either in American-owned garment factories, Hong Kong factories or at home. This labor pool has proved to be a significant factor in the revitalization of the garment industry in the metropolitan areas of New York, San Francisco, and Los Angeles.

Some Chinese have bought or rented vacated factories; others toil in these factories for long hours and terrible wages. The increased pool of unemployed seamstresses is a source of cheap labor for new garment factory owners. The garment contractors, in competition with each other, offer unrealistically low bids to get orders from manufacturers. As a result, the owners' profits often become so marginal that sometimes they cannot pay their workers at all. In San Francisco alone, several garment factories have closed because of this kind of unrealistic bidding, and some workers are owed wages which cannot be collected from factory owners. Labor unions have been called in to collect the wages from manufacturers, and in some cases they have been successful.

Many newly arrived immigrants who badly need money continue to work for low wages in garment factories. Various Chinese immigrant rights organizations have attempted to organize protests, demonstrations and labor unions. Recently, a bill was introduced in the California Assembly to prohibit manufacturers from soliciting unreasonably low bids from garment factory owners.

Because many Chinese women know how to sew, it has not been difficult to recruit skilled seamstresses from among the new immigrants. Those who do not arrive knowing how to sew learn in the garment factories here. Many factors lead Chinese women to seek employment in the factories, among them a lack of proficiency in English that limits opportunities for employment in the larger society. Another factor is the convenient location of garment factories: of the 350 garment factories in San Francisco, 100 are located in the Chinatown area. The convenient location allows Chinatown mothers to take their children to school in the mornings, have lunch with them at noon, and shop in Chinatown grocery stores after work.

The opportunity structure in the garment industry is such that opening a garment factory is within the reach of many new immigrants. Depending on the size of the factory, an initial investment varies from $40,000 to $100,000. Immigrants often pool savings from relatives and friends to start a sewing shop. Some wealthier new immigrants, such as those with Hong Kong financial ties, are able to buy a garment factory with their own cash.

Because garment factories are only contracting firms, they have little control over production. Work output varies throughout the year and volume depends on the needs of large manufacturers. In terms of production, there are two basic methods. One is the whole garment method, where the entire garment is assembled by one worker. In the second—the section method, each worker produces only one section of a garment in an assembly line fashion. Some garment factory owners in San Francisco also deliver materials to home workers. In most of the shops, workers are paid by the piece, so their salaries depend on their skills and speed. The average weekly pay is $150, although it can go as high as $200 for very efficient workers. Many workers put in extra hours to maximize their income. Some factories have instituted an hourly wage system and basic health care benefits, with productivity and efficiency in mind. Unskilled workers generally are not hired by these factories.

In a sense, the garment factory business, for both employers and employees, is a transitory business. Only first generation immigrants work in the factories: individuals in the second and third generation have no interest in the industry. Many garment factory owners, after accumulating sufficient profits, sell their business to do something else. Reasons for the high turnover in ownership probably have to do with the enormously long working hours and the intense competition among subcontractors. For many, working in a garment factory is a temporary job to save money or a transition into a better, more stable job. For instance, in the process of accumulating the necessary capital to start their own business, members of a family might each work separately, some in garment factory positions; later, they will pool their resources to set up on their own.

There are successes and failures among both employers and employees. Cinderella stories can be found, and scandals sometimes break out. A recent well-publicized scandal involved the Raymond Kong garment factories, where the owner owed workers back wages because he had misused investments and embezzled medical insurance monies. Nevertheless, garment factory businesses are still an important avenue for the realization of the "American Dream" for many Chinese immigrants who do not speak English. The story of Judy illustrates this route to the good life in America.

A Seamstress's Career.   Judy was the director of a kindergarten with 300 children in mainland China. She came to the United States in 1989. Because she could not speak English and held no United States teaching credentials, Judy could not work in American schools. Four days after her arrival in San Francisco, she located a job in a Chinese garment factory. She had never sewn before, so she was given the task of attaching buttons to newly-made clothes. Her job was quite risky as the machine used for sewing buttons could be tricky and was potentially dangerous. In the beginning, Judy was bullied by the other seamstresses who considered her clumsy and inexperienced. Additionally, her rate of pay was low. Judy found her job demeaning and she felt socially isolated in the factory. One day a co-worker accidentally discovered that Judy could write beautiful Chinese characters and could speak excellent Mandarin and Cantonese. The co-worker inquired about Judy's past career and discovered that Judy's husband was a head engineer in mainland China and that Judy herself was an educator. After this, the Chinese seamstresses started to respect her and to periodically ask her to write letters in Chinese for them (many of the Chinese seamstresses in Judy's factory could not read or write Chinese characters). Judy became included and even invited to share her co-workers' lunches. One of Judy's supervisors was also very kind to her: when the garment factory closed a few years later, Judy was able to obtain another job in a non-Chinese garment factory through the assistance of her supervisor. After two years, the factory was relocated to Mexico and Judy lost her job once again. But again through colleagues, Judy was able to find another job as a quality control person inspecting garments, a job she has held for over six years.

Working in garment factories has thus become Judy's career. She told me that she had never expected to be a garment factory worker, but now she has no ambition other than to some day open her own small garment factory with friends. Two years ago Judy's entire family was able to join her in the United States, and recently Judy became a U.S. citizen. When I asked her whether she regretted coming to America, Judy replied: "I am glad to be here. Now I have my freedom and I don't have to worry about the political problems and movements in China.... Now I can live peacefully in America with my family."

Grocery Stores

The increase in the Chinese population since 1965, and the growing number of Chinese restaurants, has benefited the grocery business in San Francisco. Today, there are about 200 Chinese grocery stores in the Bay Area. Of this number, 120 are in Chinatown or its vicinity. On Saturdays and Sundays, Chinese shoppers come from as far away as Oakland, San Rafael, Sonoma, and Palo Alto to buy their groceries in Chinatown where the prices are said to be lower.

The Chinese grocery business is very complex in that it requires domestic as well as international connections. San Francisco's Chinatown grocery stores are related to many other grocery stores in Chinatowns located throughout Canada and the United States. Since San Francisco is situated at the Pacific Rim, San Francisco's Chinatown is a distribution center for the West

Coast in Chinese dried goods. Many of the ingredients necessary for Chinese cooking are imported from China, Taiwan, Canada, Hong Kong, Mexico, and Japan. Thus for instance, a San Francisco grocery store might get mushrooms from Japan, ginseng from Wisconsin, China, and Korea, Chinese sausages from Canada, shark fins from Mexico, tea from China, fresh produce and fruits from farmers in California and soy and oyster sauces from Hong Kong and China. A store can import directly or obtain imported products through local distributors and importers. Many grocery stores team up with local bakers, importers and food processing plants. Some get their goods from the bigger grocery stores at wholesale prices.

Gift Shops and Jewelry Stores

There are about 80 gift shops and 40 jewelers in San Francisco's Chinatown. The jewelry and gift trades are interconnected. Jewelry stores sell watches, jade, and gold items which can be purchased for personal use or as gift items. Some Chinese customers purchase gold rings, chains and other valuables for decoration, for investment or as hedges against inflation.

Favorable attitudes toward China in recent years have stimulated American interest in Chinese crafts and gifts. As a tourist center, Chinatown has a steady flow of customers who purchase souvenirs, mostly imported from Hong Kong, Taiwan, and China (though some gift items are manufactured or assembled in San Francisco). The gift stores also supply materials to decorate Chinese restaurants. The gift shops further aid the neighborhood by employing Chinese housewives to assemble jewelry and gift items, and by selling locally made items such as tee shirts.

Banking, Real Estate, Hotels, and International Trading

Some new immigrants have been quick to seize opportunities to develop financing and banking institutions, as well as real estate companies, to serve the growing Chinese community, particularly wealthier immigrants looking for stable investments outside of Asia. In the 1980s many wealthy Chinese from Hong Kong bought commercial real estate in major American cities such as New York, Los Angeles, and San Francisco. Some of my informants estimated that the Hong Kong Chinese own as much as one tenth of downtown San Francisco. In the Chinese community, there is a saying that Hong Kong Chinese already own Vancouver, half of San Francisco, half of Toronto and part of New York City. While this estimate is no doubt an exaggeration, it indicates Chinese immigrants' interest in the purchase of property.

Even among middle-class Chinese, home ownership is an important goal. Homes are often purchased with the joint savings of an entire family. In recent years the ownership of property among the Chinese has increased phenomenally. According to my informants in the real estate business, middle-class immigrant families are typically able to buy a house in three to five years after immigration. As a result, ownership of property is relatively high among the new immigrants.

The wave of Chinese immigrants buying real estate has led to a proliferation of Chinese banks (Wong 1994). While ten years ago there were only three Chinese-owned banks in California, today there are thirty. In San Francisco alone, there are at least ten Chinese banks. These banks serve not only the rich, but also other, less privileged Chinese immigrants. Some of the Chinese banks publish information in Chinese to help newly arrived immigrants. For example, the United Savings Bank in San Francisco produces a pamphlet advising new immigrants on the procedures for getting a driver's license, renting an apartment, filing taxes, getting a loan, establishing a checking account, and obtaining a credit card or mortgage.

Property purchase among the new immigrants has also led to the formation of many Chinese financial companies, real estate brokerage firms, and contracting companies. There are more than ten Chinese financial companies in San Francisco specializing in real estate loan mortgages and mortgage brokering. The Chinese Business Directory of San Francisco lists sixty real estate companies. In addition, Chinese contractors, carpenters and plumbers have become visible in Chinatown and other Chinese neighborhoods in the city. Chinese house repairers, painters, landscapers, and other construction personnel are sought after by Chinese immigrant property owners who often feel more comfortable dealing with Chinese who speak their language. In addition, there seems to be a belief that Chinese business people will charge other Chinese less for the same work. Twenty years ago there were hardly any Chinese contractors; today there are at least forty Chinese contracting companies in the city of San Francisco. Many ethnic businesses, especially Chinese restaurants, hire Chinese contractors to do remodeling and landscaping. Home ownership and ethnic businesses have thus stimulated the growth of the construction trade and the real estate business in San Francisco.

New Chinese immigrants also have pursued a variety of business strategies in the United States that have drawn them into relationships and partnerships with other Asians and with white Americans. In San Francisco government officials and successful businessmen from the People's Republic of China have invested in commercial real estate, particularly in the hotel business. Many new immigrants are facilitators and conduits for these real estate transactions. In looking for secure investments, Hong Kong and Taiwan businessmen prefer to invest in shopping centers and office buildings located in busy downtown areas. They also look to invest in stable and profitable private businesses in products ranging from gifts to computers. Hong Kong businessmen are particularly interested in financing local Chinese firms which may require capital for expansion. In fact, such investments are an immigration strategy: through them, individuals may qualify for investment visas. Asian investment has been instrumental in saving many San Francisco businesses from bankruptcy and has, in the past few years, helped to sustain many businesses during California's economic recession.

There are a few wealthy immigrants from Hong Kong or Taiwan who have no need to work in the ethnic economy to get established. Labeled as the "New Money Elite" (*San Francisco Examiner,* August 20, 1989), these wealthy Hong Kong immigrants own many posh downtown office buildings in San Francisco. They have purchased, among other things, expensive clothing chains such as ACA Joe and The North Face. There are also highly skilled immigrants who are quick to seize available economic opportunities. An example is Hong Kong immigrant Vincent Tai, an architect by training, who saw a run down and underleased building in San Francisco's China Basin district. Realizing its potential, Tai quickly purchased the building for $21 million in 1979 with rich partners from Hong Kong. After entirely renovating the building, he sold it for $47 million three years later.

Similar successes are found among wealthy Chinese who remain in Hong Kong but send family members to the United States. Hotel tycoons Mr. Chan Chak-fu and Liu Che Woo, of Hong Kong, are an example. Both own hotel chains with establishments in the United States and both sent their children to be educated in the United States. Mr. Chan's son Lawrence studied hotel management at the University of Denver and Mr. Liu's son Lawrence studied structural engineering at the University of California at Berkeley and at MIT. Both sons stayed in the United States to manage their parents' hotel businesses. Lawrence Chan is president and CEO of Park Lane, which owns hotels around the world, including the Parc 55 in downtown San Francisco. Lawrence Liu runs the Holiday Inn Crowne Plaza in Burlingame and is planning to build a 25,000 square foot retail center and restaurant in San Francisco's popular South of Market neighborhood. These two examples illustrate that many new immigrants have both money and talent, and not all have to depend on the ethnic economy to survive. Nor do all new immigrants live in Chinatown. The affluent Chinese prefer to live in Hillsborough, a wealthy neighborhood in San Mateo County, an area with a more moderate climate than San Francisco. Hillsborough boasts well-built houses, some with large gardens and swimming pools. The selling prices for most of the houses in the Hillsborough area start at $1 million.

There are bankers among the ranks of the Hong Kong immigrants as well. Global Savings, Liu Chong Hang Bank, and United Savings Bank are just a few examples of banks capitalized by Hong Kong companies and families. The CEO of United Savings Bank, which has many branches in San Francisco, is an immigrant from Hong Kong who studied at San Jose State and Golden Gate Universities.

Thus, in terms of class and other factors, the new immigrants are a very heterogeneous group. Some new immigrants are *Lo Pan* (employers/capitalists), others are *Da Kung* (employees). Immigrants who live and work in Chinatown tend to be confined to the area due to their lack of English skills and capital resources, and many are involved in the ethnic economy. The wealthier new immigrants generally do not live in Chinatown and are not dependent on the ethnic economy. These bankers, capitalists, and rich hoteliers do not, it must be emphasized, represent the majority of the new immigrants. The stereotype of the rich Chinese buying up all the good real estate in the Bay Area is another exaggeration that does not apply to the typical Chinese immigrant. The majority of the new Chinese immigrants are employed as waiters or seamstresses, as professionals or laborers, and many run small family businesses.

ENGINEERS, EDUCATORS, AND ENTREPRENEURS

At least 13,000 Chinese immigrants in the San Francisco Bay Area work as professionals. They are employed by scientific and educational institutions and by various companies, and some are self-employed. In every Bay Area university, there are Chinese professors. The University of California at Berkeley, Stanford University, San Francisco State University, the University of California at San Francisco, the University of San Francisco, Santa Clara University, and a host of other institutions in the area have Chinese immigrants working as professors, medical doctors, researchers, or librarians. The University of California at Berkeley Chancellor, Chang-Lin Tien, is an immigrant from Taiwan. Nobel Prize winner Y. T. Lee worked at U. C. Berkeley for many years. One of San Francisco State University's past presidents Chia-Wei Woo was born in mainland China and educated in Hong Kong and the United States.

Proportionately, there are a large number of Chinese professionals working in Silicon Valley in computer and high-tech businesses. The 1990 census indicates that of 12,790 Chinese professionals in the five county area of San Francisco, 7,007 worked in the county of Santa Clara, where many high-tech and engineering companies are situated. In this group immigrants from Taiwan and Hong Kong outnumbered those from China. Many of these immigrants, after obtaining a Ph.D. or other advanced graduate degree, got their visa status adjusted to stay in the United States permanently.

Although Chinese professionals tend to be highly trained, they are not free from discrimination. A number of Chinese professionals have learned that certain barriers hinder their professional upward mobility. Chinese have to excel simply to get employed, and employment does not guarantee success or promotion. The phenomenon of the glass ceiling is frequently cited as an obstacle preventing Chinese professionals from advancing to higher levels in companies. It is like an unpenetrable glass; one can look up but cannot go through—upward mobility is blocked.

Because so many new immigrants are highly educated and successful, the Chinese have been labeled the "model minority," a label that has negative implications. While it is true that the overall economic performance of the Chinese in the United States is impressive, not all Chinese are so successful. It is wrong to label the entire Chinese American population a model minority. The label has been used to pit minority against minority, and what is more, Chinese have been discriminated against on the basis of the model minority label: why hire or admit Chinese when they are already such a successful group?

Betty Tung, who came to the United States from Taiwan in 1981, is a professional who has encountered discrimination in employment. After obtaining a Ph.D. in chemistry from an American university, Betty got a one year visa to practice her profession in a pharmaceutical factory. The pay, however, was not good. After one year, Betty was able to get a work visa. She told me that she was being paid less than her white male counterparts who did not have Ph.D. degrees. Betty moved from one job to another until, finally, she was able to find a company that recognized her talent and has paid her equitably. When asked why she did not return to Taiwan to find a job, Betty confided that she was worried about the future of Taiwan.

Some Chinese professionals feel that because of the subtle prejudice they encounter in the United States, their opportunities will be limited if they work in companies run by non-Chinese. As a result, a good number of professionals prefer to start business of their own. Instead of confining themselves to one location, some conduct their businesses on a global scale, finding opportunities overseas in places like China, Taiwan, South Africa, and Latin America.

The Story of Mr. Lee.   Born in Taiwan in 1956, Mr. Lee came to the United States when he finished college at the National University of Taiwan. After obtaining his Ph.D. at a well-known American university in 1985 at age twenty-nine, he got a number of job offers in Texas and California. His major professor advised him to accept a job offered by a software company in the Santa Clara area. It was his first job and he had no experience in salary negotiation. According to Mr. Lee, he made about $7,000 per year less than white engineers. Like many recent immigrants, Mr. Lee believed that through hard work he would eventually gain recognition from his employer and improve his earnings. His immediate goal was to settle quickly into life in America. His children were enrolled in an elementary school and his wife was working as an accountant and taking care of their newly purchased family home in Santa Clara.

After six years of hard work, Mr. Lee did not see much financial improvement in his job. Convinced that he had encountered the glass ceiling, he decided to look for jobs outside of the United States. During this time Taiwan had experienced rapid economic growth, and a computer company there was wooing Mr. Lee to take a position with them. After much debate and consultation with his family, Mr. Lee decided to accept the job in Taiwan. Mr. Lee explained that it was simply too good an offer to refuse. However, Mrs. Lee and the children were to remain in America. Deciding that they were committed to making Santa Clara their permanent home, a compromise was worked out where Mr. Lee would return to Taiwan only temporarily, returning home to California as often as possible.

Over the past four years, Mr. Lee has been working in Taiwan and commuting back to Santa Clara several times per year to see his family. His salary is good, but the personal and family sacrifices Mr. Lee is forced to make are high. His hope is that in another year or two, he will be able to find a better situation in the United States. He hopes to either start his own business or find another job in a local computer software company.

Mr. Lee is a good example of one of the many new Chinese immigrants who employ global strategies in their economic pursuits. The economic activities of many new immigrants are global in the sense that they transcend national boundaries. The world is their economic arena.

Mr. Lee's story is quite typical of many Chinese immigrant professionals who come to the United States for education and work possibilities, but find that they are forced to return to Asia for better work opportunities, often leaving families and children behind in the Bay Area. Many still believe that their children will have a better chance of getting into universities in the United States than in Taiwan or Hong Kong because of severe competition and limited slots for admissions there. This practice of leaving children behind and flying back and forth for professional opportunity has become a noticeable trend. Some call these global businessmen "astronauts." (*New York Times* February, 21, 1995; *Time* November 21, 1994). The *San Jose Mercury News* (August 22, 1993) estimated that 30 percent of Taiwanese immigrant engineers who work in the Silicon Valley return to Taiwan for better opportunities. Many of my informants estimated that at least a fourth of the Hong Kong immigrant professionals return to their country of origin as well.

Census data for the San Francisco Bay Area for 1990 indicate that Chinese immigrants tend to receive lower salaries as compared to the white population. One organization, Chinese for Affirmative Action, claims that few Chinese immigrants have administrative or supervisory positions in higher education or in the city, state, or federal governments. Chinese immigrants I spoke with were unhappy with what they saw was as a reluctance to promote them to supervisory levels. Various large corporations employ Chinese individuals, but few Chinese reach high-level positions: in the corporate world, there are few Chinese CEOs. Although many Chinese have received advanced educational degrees, certain obstacles to promotion continue to exist. Immigrants I interviewed complained of their in between status in America, neither black nor white. They are not promoted as frequently as African Americans through affirmative action programs, yet neither are they considered as desirable as white executives. Chinese professionals are perceived as unaggressive and lacking in verbal skills. Such prejudices and stereotypes die hard; many immigrants I spoke with had experienced this kind of prejudice first hand.

Many Chinese professionals are fighting back by filing complaints with appropriate government agencies or Chinese civil rights organizations, or by changing jobs or starting their own businesses, or returning to Asia (at least temporarily) to find better employment opportunities.

In summation, the new Chinese immigrants in the San Francisco Bay Area have responded to the economic challenges of today's modern world in three different ways. One way is by concentrating on obtaining jobs in the established ethnic niche composed of typical Chinese businesses, especially Chinese restaurants, grocery stores, garment factories, jewelry shops, and gift shops. Another way is by obtaining employment within the white establishment. This is often the case for Chinese professionals and others who can speak English well. The third way is by pursuing a global strategy, such as seeking employment or starting a business abroad. There is also a small group of new immigrants who are very wealthy and do not have to depend on the ethnic economy or gain employment from the larger United States society.

These wealthy immigrants have moved their family fortunes from Hong Kong or Taiwan to participate in the mainstream economy of the United States, for instance in banking, commercial real estate and hotel businesses. However, these Chinese are only a small minority among the new immigrants.

Contrary to the contention of those who claim that immigrants are the hapless victims of their social circumstances, Chinese newcomers are decision makers and, to a certain extent, shapers of their own destinies. Obviously, discrimination and societal barriers do exist, but the new Chinese immigrants actively devise strategies and seek solutions to counter the many obstacles facing them in their new homeland.

Whether they work in the ethnic enclave or the professional sector, the new Chinese immigrants are eager to improve their lives in the United States. For the new Chinese immigrants it is not just a place to reap financial reward, it is also a politically safe place where they can make their homes.

Family and Traditional Values: The Bedrock of Chinese Business

Many scholars have argued that family ties, especially extended family ties are detrimental to economic development. The argument is that nepotism and other familial obligations inhibit incentives to seek improvement and that mutual dependence and pressures to maintain harmonious relations within the family discourage entrepreneurial pursuits. However, recent studies of entrepreneurship among the Chinese in Hong Kong, Seychelles (Benedict 1979), Singapore (Chan and Chiang 1994), the Philippines (Amyot 1973), San Francisco (Wong, McReynolds and Wong 1992) and New York (Wong 1987a) indicate that the Chinese family plays a crucial role in Chinese business.

In traditional China social mobility could be achieved through the civil service route: a scholar-official could bring economic improvement to the family and thus glorify his ancestry. In the immigrants' world success in business can similarly glorify one's ancestry. Among Chinese immigrants the pressure to succeed is enormous: success gives one's family "face" and shows fellow countrymen and women that one's immigration venture was not in vain. Family honor and personal pride are strong motivational factors. "No one would like to cause the loss of face to one's family" and "One must try to glorify one's ancestry" are Chinese sayings that many immigrants employ to voice their concerns. Another saying, "If not successful, why immigrate?" demonstrates the constant psychological pressure to succeed. In practice an immigrant must depend on his or her family for financial and emotional support in a strange land. Indeed, family ties are critical in the Chinese ethnic economy.

Although some larger restaurants, banks, and hotels are owned and operated by wealthy, nonfamily corporations based in Hong Kong or Taiwan, according to my informants' estimates, these businesses represent only about five percent of Chinese-owned firms in the Bay Area. Family owned businesses are much more common. One of my informants, a banker in San Francisco's Chinatown and a recognized community historian, estimated that 90 percent of Chinatown businesses are family firms (including firms owned by United States-born Chinese as well as immigrants). Which family members are involved in family firms vary. Often, family firms are run by members of a nuclear, stem or extended family, but quite a few are run by other kinsmen, such as a paternal or maternal uncle along with a nephew's or niece's nuclear family. There are also firms which are run by people who came from the same village, hometown or even school in China. Hometown mates, village mates or schoolmates are sometimes treated as fictive kin.

THE ROLE OF KINSHIP IN CHINESE BUSINESS

The family firm has numerous advantages: (1) ease of training family members in business operations; (2) control of information or trade secrets; (3) family members will put in long hours; (4) families are important sources of financing; and (5) kinsmen constitute an important labor pool. In addition to these advantages, Chinese family firms offer the flexibility needed for business survival. This is particularly important in situations with keen competition and fluctuating demands for goods and services like the garment industry. Given the seasonal nature of San Francisco's garment industry, family-run factories tend to have greater endurance and flexibility than others. When business is slow, family members can do the work themselves and cut down on outside help. In adverse situations, family members can forgo a salary temporarily, or reduce the profit for each garment. Low profit margins and reduced production costs in the family firm environment have enabled many Chinese garment factories to survive during slow seasons. Family firms have many of the same benefits in the restaurant trade. In the past several years, Chinese restaurants in the Bay Area have been affected by two major events: the earthquake of 1989 and an economic recession. The reduction of tourists and local customers has caused bankruptcy among some Chinese restaurants. However, family-run Chinese restaurants have been able to survive California's economic recession.

Family firms in the Bay Area today are of three types: (1) firms owned and managed by the nuclear family; (2) firms owned and managed by siblings; and (3) firms owned and managed by a core group of kinsmen with the help of outsiders.

Family Firms Owned and Managed by the Nuclear Family

Firms run by a husband and wife and their children are normally small in size. The nuclear family in this case is both the consumption and production unit. Family members usually are paid only what is needed for daily necessities, and children help out after school or on weekends. Those who work in the firm have meals together in the common kitchen. Eating together saves manpower since one person can do the cooking and shopping. Communal eating also saves money because costly equipment is purchased together and food can be bought in bulk. This kind of family firm can maximize labor resources since everyone who can help will work in the firm. Family businesses also minimize expenditures by not hiring outsiders. Money saved can be used in a flexible manner, such as for the expansion of the business or the purchase of common properties like automobiles and houses.

Authority is structured according to the Chinese kinship system, by generation, age, sex, and birth rank. The family head, usually the oldest effective male, is the major decision maker, although adult children are allowed to make minor decisions without consultation. The division of labor is relatively simple. Day-to-day routine business operations are delegated to family members. Trust permeates the family firm. A mistake by a son or a daughter is tolerated; he or she will be given another chance and is expected to learn from the mistake. The following case gives a sense of how this kind of family business operates.

Mr. Yee and His Restaurant. Mr. Yee was born in China but moved to Hong Kong in the 1970s. In 1975, he was sponsored by his sister to come to the United States. He came with his wife and they rented a room in a rooming house in San Francisco's Chinatown. It was another five years before the Yees' three children could join them in San Francisco. Like many new immigrants, Mr. Yee worked in a Chinatown restaurant at first as a waiter. There he saved his money and learned how to operate a Chinese restaurant. His wife got a job working in a garment factory. Meanwhile, Mr. Yee instructed his children in Hong Kong to learn cooking skills and arranged for them to learn English through an adult education program organized by the Catholic church there. After his children arrived in the United States in 1980, Mr. Yee pooled the family resources and purchased a restaurant. He converted the establishment into a Cantonese seafood restaurant. Mr. Yee is the manager and his wife is in charge of the kitchen. All three sons work in the kitchen as chef, assistant chef, and dishwasher. His two daughters-in-law wait tables. It is a true family operation. None of the children plan to go to college. For them the restaurant business is seen as the avenue to achieve the American Dream. When I asked the children why they were interested in the restaurant business, one of the sons told me: "For us who do not have training in science or technology and who have no university education in America, what else can you do? This is our only way to make a living." When I asked whether they have any plans for expansion, the youngest son told me: "We have to build our foundation first. We have to do well in this family business. We have to save more money and learn more about the business. Yes, I think there is a possibility to open another one."

In most cases, the second generation Chinese immigrants are not interested in a career in the restaurant business, despite their immersion in the business from an early age. For example, one family from Taiwan started their restaurant when their children were very young. The children would go to the restaurant every day after school: the family workplace was also their playground. After eating dinner they would return home to do their homework. Now those children are teenagers, and they come to the restaurant only on weekends to help with business. The children have no interest in continuing the family business. The son, now a senior in high school, told me that the restaurant business is too hard. He hopes to find work as a computer scientist in Silicon Valley.

Family firms share common traits. They use kinship relationships for business purposes. Family members are employees, workers, and managers of the family business, and family relationships are intertwined with business relationships. Chinese immigrant family firms are a means to generate family wealth and to lay a foundation for future business ventures. Family businesses are tied to the quest for the American Dream—immigrants involved in them feel that family businesses are the only viable path to social mobility in America. Immigrants are driven to succeed in their new land. "We have spent so much time and energy in our immigration to the United States," one informant told me. "It is a loss of face if we fail in our quest for a better life." Another immigrant put it this way: "Our family business is our only avenue to a better life in America. There is no other method!" In the family firm environment, the ideology of success and the necessity of hard work are deeply ingrained in family members.

Family Firms Owned and Managed by Siblings

As a result of the Immigration Act of 1965, adult siblings of United States citizens became eligible for immigration to the United States. Quite a number of family businesses in the Chinese population are now organized around a sibling group. Compared to family firms owned by the nuclear family, those owned by siblings draw on a larger group of kinsmen, and the father is generally absent. Normally, sibling-based family firms are larger in size than nuclear family-based firms and workers are often hired from outside the family as well. Among siblings who are partners in a family business, the older brother usually acts as the leader or supervisor, though in modern America, the eldest sister might take charge. The leader organizes the family business and delegates responsibilities. He or she must have management abilities and English skills as the Yuan family firm example shows.

Ms. Yuan and Her Three Brothers. In 1989 Ms. Yuan, at the age of twenty-seven, came from Hong Kong to the United States with three brothers, ages twenty-one, twenty-three, and twenty-five. They were all born in China but grew up in Hong Kong. Their parents had been in the United States for many years. The father had died years ago, but through the sponsorship of their mother, they were all able to come to the United States.

When the Yuan children first arrived in San Francisco, they all worked in garment factories, positions they found through classified ads in the Chinese newspapers. They rented a large house in the Sunset District. In order to maximize savings, meals were taken together; rent and common expenditures were shared; and all four siblings gave their monthly paychecks to their mother, who paid the bills and put the rest of the money into a common account. After two years of hard work, the family had saved a substantial amount of money. Ms. Yuan, the oldest sibling, had the idea to organize a garment factory of their own. At the urging of their mother, all of the siblings pooled their resources and purchased a garment factory in Chinatown. The shop had only about ten sewing machines, enough to operate as a garment subcontracting firm. Meanwhile, as insurance all four siblings maintained their other jobs.

Thus the Yuans worked for others and at the same time owned their own garment factory. They paid workers by the piece and during the peak season, gave skilled and trustworthy workers take-home work as well. The little garment factory did quite well. Soon, the family was able to purchase some used machines from bankrupt factories and lend them out to seamstresses for take-home work, usually older immigrants and mothers who could not leave home for work.

Meanwhile, again at the urging of their mother, the three brothers and their sister pooled their resources to buy a modest family home in the Sunset District. To meet the needs of a family of seven, the Yuans converted the basement and the garage of their new home into bedrooms. Their plan was to stay together in this house until they had saved enough money to buy a larger house. In 1993 they were able to do just that, and recently they acquired yet a third house. Their plan now is to purchase one more home so that all four siblings and their families have individual homes.

Because the California recession has hit the garment industry quite hard, the Yuan family has discontinued take-home work in recent years. If the economic climate improves, the Yuans plan to quit their jobs and buy one larger factory to be run by all four siblings. They told me that they do not plan to continue to operate their business in Chinatown forever. They are looking for a better site in the Mission District of San Francisco. So far they have not found a suitable factory.

Family Firms Owned and Managed by Kinsmen and Outsiders

In my research I have not come across firms owned by lineages or clans. However, large family firms often hire patrilineal relatives (such as paternal uncles or cousins) or members of a family name association (who, in actuality, may not be blood relatives). This type of family firm is usually so large that it may not be able to function without the help of outsiders. The Hunan Garden (a pseudo-name) is one such example.

The Hunan Garden. This restaurant was started in 1968 by a man who came to the United States from China via Taiwan. Mr. Huang was born in China, but moved to Taiwan in 1949. He was college educated and found employment in a foreign establishment in San Francisco. When his tour of duty ended, his wife insisted that he adjust his visa and stay in the United States. The couple started a small Hunan restaurant in Chinatown. Three years later, the small restaurant had generated a substantial amount of savings. Mrs. Huang then persuaded her husband to purchase an old warehouse in downtown San Francisco and renovate it into a larger restaurant. Both husband and wife can cook, but there are very few Hunan chefs in San Francisco. The Huangs found chefs by sponsoring relatives from Hunan to come to San Francisco, and by training locals to cook Hunan cuisines.

The restaurant now has four branches and all do a brisk business. Since the principal personnel in the restaurant are relatives and students, they all feel obligated to Mr. and Mrs. Huang to work hard. Woven into the employer–employee relationship are patron–client and teacher–student relations. Business relationships are thus intertwined with kinship and friendship. Entering the restaurant, customers sense the friendliness and dedication of the manager and his staff. The food is tasty and the service is good. The restaurant has received awards from many restaurant magazines. According to both Mr. and Mrs. Huang, their success had lot to do with the dedicated assistance of their kinsmen and students.

Personal and family savings seem to be the basis for business financing among the first generation Chinese (see also Chan and Cheung's 1985 study of Chinese businesses in Toronto, Canada). The informal credit associations or rotating credit associations (hui) of old, as described by Light (1972), B. Wong (1982) and others, in which members made contributions to a fund given to the highest bidder, are now an insignificant source of financing among new immigrant entrepreneurs. Nor is it common for Chinese immigrants to borrow money from banks to finance business ventures. According to one prominent Chinatown banker, all banks consider loans for small start-up businesses too risky. When it is necessary to borrow money, families usually mortgage their homes to obtain cash to start a business.

Pooling family resources adds an extra dimension of solidarity and responsibility to business enterprises. One informant stated: "I can't start or manage the business myself. I need my family members to help me. We pull our money together and everyone in the family feels responsible for the business. It feels closer to do business with family members. We all have the same stake in the business. We are business partners, associates and at the same time we are family."

There is a developmental cycle of family firms so that many start out with members of a nuclear family and expand to include extended kin. According to an argument put forward by S. L. Wong (1985), business partnerships between unrelated Chinese immigrants often lead to family firms. Unrelated business partners sometimes pool resources because their families do not have sufficient resources to help them. Once the partnership amasses enough financial strength, an extended family businesses can emerge, although nonkin partnership arrangements often disintegrate before this stage because of differences of opinion, accusations of embezzlement, and other conflicts.

FAMILY MEMBERS AS EMPLOYERS AND EMPLOYEES

If enough family members are available to fill the jobs in a Chinese firm, they are the preferred individuals to hire. However, the practice of hiring outsiders is common among Chinese family firms and appears to be on the rise. Both regionalism and dialect similarities are important considerations in hiring. Taiwanese prefer to hire Taiwanese just as the mainland Chinese and the

Hong Kong Chinese prefer their compatriots. Nonfamily employ-ees are usually brought in because of the need for special talents and skills that no family member possesses, such as cooking experience or knowledge of herbs. Sometimes family firms hire outsiders because the family's children have taken better paying positions in the American job market and are not interested in working in the family business.

Small family firms such as hardware or electronic stores are often simply run by a husband and wife. However, larger opera-tions often need to hire help from outside the family. Grocers often hire outsiders to manage stock. A chef who is not a member of the family may be given a partnership in a restaurant to encourage his commitment to the business. Similarly, a Chinese herb store may need to hire an outside specialist. Garment factories require many employees and usually use outsiders as seamstresses, though supervisory positions may be held by family members. Even non-Chinese at times are hired for essential positions which cannot be filled by family members or kinsmen. Common exam-ples are managers of banking or financing operations. A trend among Chinese restaurants recently is the hiring of Mexican American busboys and waiters. In suburban Chinese take-out res-taurants, it is common to hire white receptionists to take orders and white drivers to do deliveries for the ease of communication.

Thus Chinese enclave businesses are no longer as isolated and culture bound as they used to be. They transcend ethnic lines in their business activities and in their competition for customers and even employees. Their businesses have become more diversi-fied and their circles of customers and employees have enlarged to include whites and other non-Chinese.

There continues to be pressure on family members to help out relatives in need by giving them jobs. Especially after they have established their own businesses, the Chinese are obligated by kinship norms to sponsor relatives from Hong Kong, Taiwan or the mainland to get visas to move to the United States. The impending transfer of the control of Hong Kong from Great Brit-ain to the People's Republic of China has further heightened expectations of sponsorship. Through the visa-sponsoring pro-cess, relationships among relatives have become even more com-plex as employers and patrons often act as sponsors. Newly arrived immigrants feel obligated to their sponsoring relatives and work hard to reciprocate the social debt they have incurred.

In Chinese family firms, family values and kinship ideology are intertwined with the values and ideology of the family business (Wong, McReynolds and Wong 1992). The traditional Chinese values of *ganqing* (sentimental feelings), *yiqi* (personal loyalty), and *renqing* (sympathy) are still highly regarded. In San Francisco's Chinatown, all but two owners of ninety-one family firms I spoke with considered these qualities important in both employer–employee and employee–customer relationships. Traditionally these values have contributed to harmonious relations by instilling feelings of commitment, responsibility, and integrity on the part of family members working together. Ideally, employers are expected to be as concerned about the welfare of the individuals who work for them as if they were family members. In turn, employees are supposed to be loyal and contribute as best they are able to the firm.

Exploitation in Chinese firms does exist. Outsiders who work in the family firms sometimes complain about (1) depressed wages, (2) long hours, (3) the lack of medical benefits, and (4) the lack of *yiqi* (personal loyalty or righteousness). Workers in Chinese garment factories who get paid by the piece complain about how they need to work long hours for a reasonable pay. In Chinese restaurants workers complain that sometimes they have to contribute part of the tips they collect to their employers. Some say that they even have to pay for what they eat in the restaurant. Occasionally, there are cases of embezzlement of workers' contribution to various insurance plans.

However, there are fewer overt conflicts between employers and employees in Chinese firms than in other business establishments in America. One seldom sees demonstrations or strikes in Chinese establishments, except in rare cases. Class conflicts are minimized due to the fact that employers often work side by side with employees. Also, employees today may be employers tomorrow. When I interviewed several employees in the garment factory owned by the Yuan family, I found that they admired the industry and frugality of their employers. When asked whether they felt they were exploited in any way, a typical answer was that "the Yuan family has the righteousness. They are working class people like we are. They really have family spirit!"

There is a great deal of personalism in the family firm environment. Workers who have personal needs or personal problems may direct them to their employers. For instance, one garment factory worker wanted her employer to find a job or a chore in the factory for her mother, who needed money and felt lonely at home. The worker also felt it would be safer for her mother to be at the factory than home alone. In this case, the employer, out of yiqi, felt he had to—and did—honor the worker's request.

In the Chinese firm environment, traditional etiquette, customs, and festivals are observed. Workers are given moon-cakes for the mid-autumn festival and *leishi* (gift money wrapped in red paper) and tangerines (symbols of luck) during the Chinese New Year. Chinese restaurant workers are often offered special dinners to celebrate the Chinese Winter Solstice Festival.

Family firms which take into consideration the personal and cultural needs of the workers tend to get high praise from their workers. Some workers feel obligated to reciprocate the employers' treatment by working hard and being loyal. In 1992 a Chinese garment factory in the San Francisco Bay Area was closed. It owed the workers back wages. The International Ladies Garment Workers (ILGWU) and a community organization went to fight for the workers. In the end the workers were able to get their back pay. However, some workers returned their checks to the owners, a move which angered the union that had fought for them.

Of course, not all employees are happy with their Chinese employers. Some occasionally resort to a number of resistance tactics, including gossiping, slowing-down, wasting materials, refusing to work extra hours, practicing speech avoidance with employers, and resisting last minute schedule changes. In severe cases, employees have voiced their protests to a labor union or a community organization. When an employer is known to lack yiqi, it can spell ruin, for he may find it difficult to retain or attract good workers who hear of him through the grapevine. Slow-downs can also be very effective, especially on Sundays or holidays in Chinese restaurants where the line of customers tends to be long. To avoid labor conflicts, many Chinese employers try to be less exploitative and to have more yiqi.

Chinese family firms operating in a traditional paternalistic fashion have sometimes been described as authoritarian or even greedy in the demands they place on family employees (Benedict 1968; Coser 1974; 1986). But these problems do not seem to be major one in the family businesses I studied, where a certain amount of egalitarianism exists among family members involved. True, the major financial contributor is the family head, and he may take advantage of the authority accorded him in Chinese tradition and make decisions independently. But even in Chinese tradition the family head is perceived as a caretaker rather than an owner of family assets. Today in firms run by husbands and wives, decision making is often shared between them. Thus, for instance, when Mr. Tang wanted to renovate the kitchen of their restaurant, he consulted his wife about what needed to be replaced and what equipment needed to be added. Since they could afford only $20,000 for the project, Mr. Tang had to compromise with his wife who wanted to do the exhaust ventilation system and a stainless steel sink first. Both husband and wife agreed that other improvement work could be postponed until they had accumulated more savings. Even in larger firms with an extended family structure, the financial and labor contributions of family members are recognized and family members are likely to be consulted about decisions.

The May-May Garment Factory. Consider the decision making process in one garment factory which was incorporated in 1970. The family head and founder of the firm is the oldest brother Tony who was sponsored to come to the United States in 1966 by his older sister who worked at a university. Tony wanted to go into business but lacked the necessary capital and skills. After he arrived, he discussed his plans with friends who advised him to go to Chinatown, where he obtained a job in a Chinese restaurant. Tony first worked as a busboy but soon got promoted to waiter because he was able to speak English, Cantonese, and Mandarin. Because he was a good worker and had good self-presentation, he was soon made the captain. While working Tony closely studied the operation of garment factories, and during his spare time he visited a few of them. He decided that he wanted to get into the garment industry, and he sent word to his three younger sisters and his fiancee in Hong Kong to learn to sew. He even subsidized their enrollment in sewing school. In 1969 Tony took a job as a garment presser in a garment factory to gain hands-on experience. Meanwhile, he sponsored his fiancee and three sisters to come to San Francisco. They were all employed as seamstresses in different garment factories. After ten months of working, they were able to pool their resources to purchase a factory. It was a joint family venture: Tony and his wife owned 60 percent of the shares, the three sisters owned 40 percent.

The firm chose the section-work or assembly-line method for garment production. Among the forty workers of the May-May Garment Factory, there were two groups of people: the core group, composed of the three sisters and Tony, and the peripheral group, consisting of nonfamily members. The brother was the major decision maker for the daily business routines. Minor business decisions were delegated to the sisters, who also served as the principal technical personnel of the firm. In internal relationships, the brother was the owner, boss, employer, and patron-protector. He considered himself protector of the family business: should he fail, the family firm would fail, and the family would fail with it.

Tony was the overall supervisor of production while his sisters were assistant supervisors who took care of several sections. In the factory, Tony took care of final products, including pressing and inspection to make sure defects had been removed or corrected. However, in bidding for bundles (orders), Tony had to consult with his sisters to get their opinion about garments and certain patterns, such as which patterns were complicated or difficult to sew. Tony knew that it was important to have a realistic estimate about labor and time required for the production of each garment before entering a profitable bid. As manager of the firm and elder brother, Tony functioned as the head of his family. He would take all of his family members out every Sunday to a Chinese restaurant and sightseeing. However, when business was good, family members were expected to forego all Sunday entertainment to work. Nonfamily employees were not expected to work on holidays because it would constitute a violation of work contracts and the union would object. Tony acted as a patron of his nonfamily employees in many ways. He was a counselor on matters such as schooling for children and obtaining drivers' licenses. He often got information for his employees on the latest immigration rulings, investments, and housing. He recommended lawyers, accountants and English tutors. His employees reciprocated by working hard and staying with the firm even during slow seasons. The factory had a mahjong table that the workers used during their free time.

After fifteen years of work, the family decided he get out of the garment business. There were simply too many Chinese garment factories competing with each other, and profit margins had declined. Tony told me that all the members of his family were dependent on the salaries from their labor at their factory. After a lengthy period of deliberation, Tony and his sisters decided to sell their garment factory while they were still ahead financially. The company was sold several years ago and the proceeds from the sale were divided. One of the sisters got married and moved out of town. The other two got together to start a boutique. Tony and his wife each own their own business now—he runs a poultry store and she has a boutique.

On the surface Tony might have appeared to be the only decision maker in the family garment factory, but a closer look shows that consultation among family members was common, especially in making major decisions such as selling the factory.

In the daily management of a small firm, such as a family run restaurant, it is typical for all able family members to contribute, with or without pay. The father may set the tables and wash the dishes. The mother and her brother may do the cooking. A son may serve as the cashier while daughters wait tables. School-aged children will fill in whenever they can. Jobs are not necessarily clearly defined, and will be performed by any family member as the need arises. In small family firms, which are most common in San Francisco outside of Chinatown and in suburban communities, the nuclear family and the economic unit are clearly one. The King Wah Restaurant in San Mateo County is an example. The son answers the telephone and takes orders from customers. He is also the waiter and manager. He bags foods for take-out customers and orders necessary ingredients from grocery stores and supermarkets. The father occasionally chops vegetables, prepares tea and functions as a busboy to clear tables. When the father is not available, the son may do these tasks. Likewise, when the son is out, the father takes on his tasks. The mother and her brother go to the restaurant early each morning to make egg fu-yung, prepare egg-rolls, cook rice, and fry pork and spare ribs in preparation for various dishes. Every day from 10:00 A.M. to 2:00 P.M., and from 4:00 P.M. to 10:00 P.M., the family cooks for customers. Between 2:00 P.M. and 4:00 P.M., they cook for themselves. The Chinese restaurant business is a labor intensive business which requires a lot of preparatory work.

A Son's Travel Agency.   Similarly, in a travel agency I studied, the owner-son Robert handled customers and airline reservations; his father took care of documentation and paperwork and his mother was in charge of accounting. The firm only hired one part-time secretary, a college student, as well as a cousin who wanted to learn about the travel business. The owner Robert learned about the travel business by working for another agency when he was a student. Both parents worked part-time: they enjoyed going to Chinatown and working with their son. When business was good Robert's parents worked longer hours. When business was slow they could go home early to do household chores or shop in Chinatown. Sometimes, when Robert needed to go out, the father would step in to help with airline reservations or to answer queries from customers. He also prepared application forms for customers applying for reentry permits to the United States. The atmosphere at the travel agency was relaxed, and work schedules were flexible. Robert's firm was not just a place to make a living, it was also a place where his parents could help out and feel needed. Thus the value of some family firms cannot be measured strictly on a monetary basis.

CONFUCIANISM, TRADITIONS, AND BUSINESS

Chinese traditions and values play a role in businesses in the Bay Area today. Indeed, many Chinese restaurants, garment factories, gift shops and even herbal stores have a statue of Guan Gung on their premises. One informant told me that the statue of Guan Gung—the patron deity of justice and wealth—was an effective motivator for the workers in her restaurant's kitchen. Her staff, facing the statue while they work, are constantly reminded of the virtue of justice. According to my informant, the staff tended to be more careful with cooking materials and less wasteful if they saw the statue of Guan Gung in the kitchen.

Confucianism, once considered by Weberian scholars to be a hindrance to economic development, is now thought to be a driving force for the economic success of the five tigers: Japan, Korea, Singapore, Hong Kong and Taiwan. Among immigrants in the San Francisco Bay Area, Confucian values of family are clearly important to Chinese firms in a number of ways. First there is the Confucian emphasis on the importance of the family as the main social unit of society. It is the moral obligation of each individual to care for his or her family. When the family is cared for, it is believed, the society and community are cared for. When the family is right, the community will be right. When the community is right, the nation will be right and when each nation is right, the world will be right. Therefore, it is important to have the family under control, socially, economically, and ethically. When the family is regulated, the community and nation can be regulated. Second, within the family, Confucian rules and discipline stress a hierarchical order, and authority is structured according to generation, age, and gender. Fathers have authority over sons; husbands over wives; and older brothers take precedence over younger ones. Many social scientists believe that this hierarchical structure meshes well with business activities, for it instills discipline and allows tasks to be assigned without confusion about the chain of command. Commitment to family can easily be translated to commitment to the family firm.

The Confucian notion of filial piety is also a factor in children's involvement in Chinese family firms. Children are taught to be respectful to their parents and to their ancestors. To be obedient to one's parents, to be solicitous to their needs, is to practice filial piety. To save family wealth and continue the family business is thought to be an obligation for children, and a form of filial piety. In the family firm environment, children who work hard and dedicate themselves to the family business are held up as examples of filial piety.

The emphasis on ancestral lineage and family continuity also is helpful for family businesses. The success of one's family will bring glory to one's ancestors. Similarly, in order to glorify one's ancestry, one must succeed in scholarship and business. It is a parents' obligation to help one's children obtain higher education, to have a successful business so that children can go to universities. This remains an overarching concern for Chinese immigrants.

The value of having face is emphasized in Chinese culture, and children in Chinese families are inculcated with the importance of face from an early age. To have face is to have honor. Not only should each individual be concerned about his or her individual honor, he or she should also be concerned about the honor of his or her family and ancestors. Thus it is important not to injure one's reputation or the reputation of one's family. For the sake of one's personal face, one has to work hard and achieve success. Individual success can gain more face for the family. For people will then say: "So and So is successful because he has been properly raised by his family." An individual's academic and financial success is thought to be due to the work of one's family and ancestors as well. For those who achieved economic success in traditional China (before 1949), it was customary to return to the homeland to purchase property to glorify their ancestors. A powerful and rich family name association is also a reflection of the economic success of its members. In the past, successful Chinese immigrants often donated large sums of money to their family name associations.

BUSINESS CONTINUITY

The question of continuity plagues all Chinese family firms in the San Francisco Bay Area no matter what their size or make up. When Chinese entrepreneurs make decisions about the future, they are influenced by traditional Chinese values as well as the social, political, and economic environment they confront in the United States. In terms of expansion, the limits of family size and a characteristic conservatism among family businesses make the decision to expand through the use of outsiders a risky one (Benedict 1968; Donckels and Frohlich 1991; F. Hsu 1981; S. L. Wong 1985).

Most Chinese family firms begun by new immigrants are relatively short-lived, rarely extending beyond one generation. Some writers have attributed the demise of family businesses in traditional China to inheritance rules that, in their ideal form, require the division of family assets equally among all male descendants. Possessions are continually divided and subdivided among offspring, making growth impossible (Hsu 1981). In the United States, other factors are more important in explaining the brief life span of Chinese family firms. Perhaps most important is the unwillingness of the second and third generations to continue working in family businesses. Because of their familiarity with the dominant American culture and their greater English abilities, members of the younger generations have more opportunity for social and economic mobility in the United States than their immigrant parents did. The United States born children often feel alienated from the traditional Chinese management style of their elders. Moreover, there are the inevitable problems of preserving discipline in the firm and obtaining an ongoing line of capable leadership.

In Chinese family firms owned by first generation immigrants, traditional values such as familism, reciprocity, sentimentality and personality are highly regarded. The firms often employ, and may even depend upon, immigrants' knowledge of their native language and culture. Meanwhile, the immigrants' children may not even speak Chinese. One informant explained:

"Look at the firm around the corner on Columbus. They have a brisk business. The firm is run by a man and his daughter. The family business has been supporting the education of other children. Now the children are grown and have found employment in American establishments. They have no intention of returning to the family business. Many Chinese family businesses are too difficult for the second generation Chinese. They have to work long hours but receive little reward. The immigrant business is good only for those who have no higher education and other economic opportunity."

The closure and sale of family businesses are not necessarily signs of failures. Some shops are sold simply because of good offers. Others close because better opportunities become available. Many family businesses that break up or are sold do so because of family conflicts, as in the case that follows.

The Family Business of Mr. and Mrs. Chung. The Chung family came to the United States in 1991. They were considered a middle-class family in Hong Kong. Their two children are college educated: one just graduated from the University of Southern California, the other is a college junior. After arriving in the United States, Mr. and Mrs. Chung both worked for a real estate developer. The pay was bad and husband and wife both decided to quit their jobs and start a small restaurant with the savings they brought with them from Hong Kong. They were excited by their new business, though initially they had to overcome many hurdles. One was attracting new customers. Another hurdle was the costly repairs that the new restaurant needed. Although they worked hard, the Chungs experienced a cash flow problem. After consulting with experts, they developed a system to minimize expenses. Instead of hiring a full time manager, Mrs. Chung became the manager, cashier, waiter, receptionist, and owner herself. Mr. Chung was the supervisor and he worked in the kitchen as a cook. Only part-time workers were hired to do delivering and to assist in cooking. Several months later, the business became prosperous. The cash flow problem was resolved, and the Chungs were each able to withdraw a salary of $2,500 per month. They ate all of their meals at the restaurant and went home only to sleep. Their biggest expense was their mortgage.

The Chungs' major problem arose not from their business but from their marriage. Mrs. Chung was happy to be in the United States, but her husband was not. Mr. Chung was unhappy because he felt that his wife had become his boss. He often felt left out because he could not speak English. There were other personal conflicts: frequent quarrels at home and disagreements at the restaurant. Once, after such a disagreement, Mr. Chung walked off his job as cook and Mrs. Chung had to replace him for the day. Mr. Chung became uncooperative, on occasion singing loudly in Chinese or shouting from the kitchen. Mrs. Chung felt that he was spoiling the family business and was an impossible husband. She asked him for a divorce. Initially Mr. Chung refused and the business and family situation further deteriorated until Mr. Chung stopped going to the restaurant altogether. Eventually, Mr. Chung agreed to the divorce and the couple sold their business. It was put up for a quick sale and the proceeds were divided according to the divorce settlement.

There are also instances of business mismanagement and miscalculations that lead to the failures of family businesses. For example, the discount store of the Wu Brothers, which was started in 1994, lasted only ten months and went bankrupt in 1995. Both brothers had come from mainland China in 1992 and, after working in Chinese restaurants as waiters for two years, they pooled $20,000 and started a discount store selling shoes, leather jackets, custom jewelry and other apparel. Once a week, one of the brothers had to drive to Los Angeles to buy their goods from wholesalers. Because of limited capital they could only rent a store in an inexpensive area in Oakland, where they paid $1,000 for about 1,000 square feet. During the day, the street where their store was located seemed safe, but after 5:00 P.M. it was not safe. The foot traffic was not good, and the surrounding neighborhoods were run-down. Business was poor from the very beginning, a problem the two brothers originally attributed to the recession in California. However, as time went on it became clear that the kinds of merchandise they were carrying were not attractive to most customers in their area. Generally, their location was not favorable for their retail business. Their daily cash did not cover expenses, and the family business was a failure. The Wu brothers closed their family business and returned to waiting tables in Chinese restaurants.

In general, Chinese family businesses which last beyond the first two years tend to endure, and some even go on to expand. Among the Chinese business owners interviewed for this study, opinions about continuity and expansion were diverse. The economic recession, the demolition of a highway providing access to Chinatown (following the 1989 earthquake) and parking and traffic problems in Chinatown have contributed to a pessimistic view of expansion prospects. Some owners reported that the loss of the highway had reduced their business by as much as 30 percent. Other owners expressed satisfaction with their existing businesses and saw no reason to expand. One said: "We just want to make a living; we should be happy with what we have." Many immigrants who operate businesses without the aid of their children plan to close their businesses when they retire, because their children have found better employment elsewhere or are not interested in continuing the family business.

However, other owners are more constrained by economic factors than the availability of family labor. Some are simply waiting for an appropriate time and until they accumulate enough capital before they make an expansionist move. These owners are often willing to hire outsiders if family members are unable or unwilling to participate in the family business. Although they prefer to work with family members, when it comes to the survival or expansion of their business, many owners are willing to do whatever is necessary, including hiring outsiders.

Global Strategies of Chinese Professionals and Businessmen

The new Chinese immigrants differ significantly from the old settlers in that many are highly educated professionals and affluent businessmen who operate on a global stage. In response to changing economic opportunity structures in the world, new immigrants have diversified from the traditional ethnic niche and professional occupations into international trade. Some have become global and transnational, conducting business in different parts of the world and producing, distributing and investing in different locales. For some new Chinese immigrants, long distance commuting has become common. Some are required by their jobs to live temporarily in one country and conduct business in another, often leaving families behind in one permanent location.

Among the new immigrants are professors working in universities in the San Francisco Bay area who also conduct their careers in a global arena. The University of California at Berkeley was headed by Chang-Lin Tien, an immigrant from Taiwan. Yuan T. Lee, a Nobel Prize winner, also worked at U. C. Berkeley for many years. In the past, San Francisco State University was presided over by Chia-Wei Woo, who was born in mainland China and educated in Hong Kong and the United States. Two of the three named above have since gone back to Hong Kong and Taiwan for better opportunities.

Yuan T. Lee came to the United States for advanced training. After he earned his Ph.D. in chemistry at U. C. Berkeley, he stayed to climb the academic ladder in the United States. In 1986 Lee won a Nobel Prize in chemistry. At the peak of his career in 1994 Dr. Lee returned to Taiwan at the age of fifty-seven to head the prestigious Academia Sinica which houses twenty-one research institutes.

This phenomenon of returning to one's country of origin has recently caught on among many new immigrants in the United States. Major newspapers in the United States have noted that some of the most distinguished immigrant scientists and professionals who have enriched the West with their talents and contributions are now returning to Asia. Although many young Chinese students and professionals continue to come to the United States for university educations and business opportunities, more and more are seeking employment in Asia where opportunities are expanding.

Chia-Wei Woo, who was recruited from San Francisco State University to become the first president of Hong Kong's new University of Science and Technology in 1988, said that it was a once in a lifetime experience to be a founder and president of a new university. Besides, the pay in Hong Kong is better than in San Francisco. With a generous fringe benefits package and a liberal housing allowance, he said: "I could not simply resist such an opportunity." However, Woo's wife and children continue to live in their permanent home in Hillsborough, near the city of San Francisco. Many scholars feel the appeal of Asia. Dr. Yuan Lee was quoted as saying: "Taiwan needs me, while to the University of California, it doesn't make that much difference whether I'm there or not." (*Time*, November 21, 1994).

The motives for returning home are complex. Some people are attracted by the new found opportunities in engineering, science, and computer design. Others are motivated by the entrepreneurial urge to start their own business. Some have felt the presence of a glass ceiling that has blocked their career advancement in United States firms. Still, many of those who return to Asia retain their American citizenship or green card as a way of keeping their global options open.

Some Chinese businessmen also fear that the economic potential of Silicon Valley is being inhibited by high costs, high wages, and low productivity. By contrast, Taiwan's economy is growing and its proximity to the burgeoning consumer markets in Asia holds better promise for the future. Further, the nagging recession of the 1990s has affected California more than many other states because California was home to the defense and aeronautics industries which were hit particularly hard. The impact of the decline of these industries has been felt on other sectors of the economy such as real estate, tourism, and retail. Small businesses, larger firms and professionals all have been affected. Many Chinese businesses have sufffered because of high unemployment rates and the accompanying loss of purchasing power of many consumers. At the same time, the economies in Asia have experienced unprecedented growth. In combination these conditions have triggered the exodus of a good many new immigrants.

THE "ASTRONAUT" TREND

Many of the new immigrants employ global strategies. They think and act in global terms rather than in national or community terms. Many recent Chinese immigrants in the San Francisco Bay Area are well-versed in current events and worldwide economic development issues. Their international exposure and training have helped them adapt to a changing world. Instead of confining their economic activities to a given locality, they have transcended national boundaries as they look for employment or conduct their economic pursuits. The Chinese use the term "astronaut" to describe people who travel, live, and work in different parts of the world as they explore opportunities in the global village. Astronauting is, in fact, an adaptive strategy recently spawned in response to corporate downsizing, research cutbacks, and recession in America in the past several years.

Mr. Fu, one informant, told me that he traveled back to China to start a joint venture there. While he was in Hong Kong, he met an old neighbor who was interested in starting a Japanese restaurant in South Africa. Fu became a part-owner by contributing one seventh of the start-up capital for the restaurant in Johannesburg. Mr. Fu now has a small import and export company in the United States, a joint venture in China and a partnership in South Africa. He has joined the ranks of the astronauts—he is neither here nor there, and his family remains in the United States.

International commuting between work in Asia and family in the Bay Area is not easy. It is hard on the children, the marriage, and the traveler. The following stories illustrate some of the problems of commuting.

Mr. Zee, a Chinese Accountant.   Mr. Zee was an accountant in Hong Kong. Fearing the uncertain future of Hong Kong after its eventual return to the People's Republic of China in 1997, Mr. Zee and his wife, who had been a teacher in Hong Kong, decided to move to the United States. After their arrival in San Francisco in 1992,

Mr. Zee spent more than six months looking for suitable employment in his field. His accounting degree from Hong Kong University could not get him any job from white accounting firms. The only job he could find was as a bookkeeper in a Chinese restaurant. After he received his green card he returned to Hong Kong for a visit and tried to win his old job back. To his surprise, Mr. Zee was welcomed back by his former employers with open arms. When I met Mr. Zee he had been working in Hong Kong for the past three years.

At the same time, Mrs. Zee continues to live in the United States and take care of their two children. When Mrs. Zee first came to the United States, she stayed home with the children, but once they began high school, she decided to look for work outside of the home. She found a job working part-time as a cashier in a Chinese firm. The entire family is reunited only twice a year. During the summer, Mr. Zee comes from Hong Kong to stay with his family for approximately two to three weeks. During the Chinese New Year, Mr. Zee again comes back to California to pay a brief visit. This family separation has created many problems in their lives. Mr. Zee's children have a hard time relating to their father because he is not around most of the time. Mrs. Zee told me that he will only continue this arrangement for two more years. Both Mr. Zee and his wife believe that he should continue to work in Hong Kong until 1997, when, the two feel, he will no longer have the opportunity to make as much money. Mr. Zee hopes that by 1997 he will have accumulated enough savings to start a business in the United States.

Mr. Yang. This astronaut life style has become a trend, especially during the last five years. As an example, the *San Jose Mercury News* (August 22, 1993) reported the experiences of the Tsenshau Yang and Samuel Liu families. Mr. Yang, an engineer in his late thirties, came to the United States from Taiwan to study. After obtaining his doctoral degree in engineering at Stanford University, he stayed to work in Silicon Valley. However, he went back to Taiwan in 1993 to work as a vice president of a start-up company designing integrated circuits. His wife Shyun and their two children still live in Cupertino. He comes back to visit his family several times a year. For him, Taiwan offers better opportunities in his field, but for his wife, an accountant, finding equivalent work in Taiwan is difficult. Mr. Yang returned to Taiwan with the blessing of his wife. She said: "I didn't want him to come to me in ten years and tell me he regretted not starting his own business.... But now, I am beginning to regret it because he's not home most of the time."

Mr. Liu. Mr. Samuel Liu, another Taiwanese engineer, had a similar experience. After receiving an American education and working as president of a Silicon Valley integrated systems firm for a number of years, Mr. Liu returned to Taiwan to take over a troubled semiconductor company which had made him an attractive job offer. Mr. Liu is able to return home about seven times a year to see his wife and children, but he misses them when he is in Taiwan. Global immigrants like Mr. Liu do indeed make sacrifices in pursuit of career advancement.

Other astronaut families are not as lucky as the three I have just described. In some, children go unsupervised and experience problems in school and at home, sometimes ending up joining gangs. Some families experience emotional and marital problems. Clearly, new immigrants often pay a high price when they lead the life of an astronaut.

GLOBAL BUSINESS STRATEGIES

In today's global economy, processes of production often span beyond national boundaries and items of consumption may be assembled in more than two countries. Modern technologies of communication and transportation have shortened the distances of international travel. Businesses located in one country are being replaced by multinational corporations run by people from different nations with branches in disparate parts of the world. Enlarging one's sphere of economic activity and developing transnational networks to capture a larger market share are business strategies employed by some Chinese immigrants.

In the 1980s multinational corporations began to be formed among new Chinese immigrants. The principal organizers of these corporations have been the rich Hong Kong Chinese who live in different parts of the world. Many of these corporations are truly globalized as partners are frequently scattered over North America, Europe, and Asia. The Chinese restaurant chain known as Harbor Village, for example, has branches in Los Angeles, Hong Kong, Kowloon, and San Francisco. Some Chinese, who have a base in the United States, have also formed multinational corporations to develop shopping centers, build residential housing and develop office buildings and other commercial real estate businesses. These corporations may involve Chinese from Hong Kong, Thailand, Taiwan, as well as the United States.

Diversifying investment in different parts of the world is common among the very rich Chinese immigrants. Thus, for instance, Alexander Lui owns Anvil International Properties, Inc. in San Francisco and acts as board director of Furama Hotel Enterprises, Ltd. in Hong Kong. Mr. Lui is also on the Board of Directors of Trans Pacific Bancorp in San Francisco. The *San Francisco Examiner* (August 21, 1989) reported that the Lui family has investments and development interests throughout Asia and Indonesia. Another example is Anthony Chan. His family has extensive investment in China and he himself has been a general partner of WorldCo., Ltd. since 1972. He and his partners developed a twelve-story office building located at 1388 Sutter Street in San Francisco. They also developed shopping centers around the Bay Area, especially in the South Bay. These Hong Kong businessmen have connections and businesses in different parts of the world. Moreover, they have personal contacts in Chinese communities in different countries. Robert Chan Hing Cheong, for example, is the former chairman of HK-TVB, a Hong Kong cable company. In his attempt to establish connections in San Francisco, he made many business trips to the city to visit his former schoolmate, Deputy Mayor James K. Ho (*San Francisco Examiner*, August 21, 1989).

Friendships as well as classmate and alumni connections have been important for Chinese businessmen. In San Francisco students from Hong Kong's Diocesan Boys School or St. Stephen are known to form strong networks. Many live in the prestigious Hillsborough community. Some also served as commissioners under former San Francisco Mayor Art Agnos. On Sundays, many of the participants in this old-boys network play basketball in their neighborhood and meet at other social functions.

Diversifying and globalizing family businesses into different fields and different locations has become a common response of wealthy Hong Kong business people to cope with trends in the modern business world. Global strategies are also a device to gradually move capital from the colony before its return to China in 1997.

The Ho Tim family, for instance, runs Honorway Investment Company, which developed the twenty-six-story office and condominium building at 388 Market Street in San Francisco. The family firm also owns the Brooks Brothers Building in popular Union Square. The family patriarch was the chairman of the Miramar Hotel in Hong Kong. His son Hamilton Ho commutes frequently between Hong Kong and San Francisco on family business. Another notable Bay Area family are the Mas, who own 456 Montgomery Street in San Francisco's Financial District, a twenty-six-story building that was built in 1985. The Ma family also owns and controls Tai Sang Land Development Company in San Francisco and Tai Sang Bank in Hong Kong. The brother is chairman of Tai Sang in Hong Kong and his sister Joy Ma is in charge of Tai Sang in San Francisco and lives in Sausalito. The Kwok Ta-seng family owns a large Chinese restaurant in Millbrae in the South Bay as well as some valuable downtown real estate in San Francisco. This family also owns a successful real estate company in Hong Kong, Sun Hung Kai Properties, Ltd. The Chan Chak-fu family owns the Parc 55 Hotel in San Francisco, the Hyatt Regency in Oakland, and the Park Lane Hotels in Hong Kong and San Francisco (*San Francisco Examiner*, August 20, 1989).

Many business tycoons are concerned with preserving family wealth and thus hire only family members to run their family businesses. Sons and daughters are the trusted helpers in dealing with transnational family enterprises. Thus, the very rich, out of economic necessity, have globalized their families along with their businesses. These are transnational families with, for instance, some members living in Hong Kong and some in the United States.

To cope with rapid global changes, some rich Hong Kong Chinese send their children to be educated in different parts of the world. Thus, for instance, the Chang family sent their oldest son William to an English boarding school and later to Harvard to study economics. Or take the Chan family's educational strategies. In addition to heavy involvement in commercial real estate in California and Nevada, the Chan family owns hotels in Hong Kong, Sydney, New York, Phoenix, Hawaii, San Antonio, and San Francisco. Lawrence Chan, who was expected to run the family's hotel business, was sent to Switzerland and then to Denver to study and prepare for a career in hotel management. International experience is thought to be important in certain businesses—and rich Hong Kong business families see globalization in a child's education as a definite advantage.

Of course, the movers and shapers of these big Chinese businesses and multinational corporations represent only a small minority of Chinese immigrants. Only about two or three dozen Chinese families in the entire Bay Area participate in this kind of large scale international business ventures. Although few in number, wealthy Chinese immigrant capitalists are key players in the global economy and possess both the power and the money to pursue global business strategies which are otherwise available only to very rich white Americans.

THE ESTABLISHMENT OF AN INTERNATIONAL TRADING NETWORK

Some new Chinese immigrants use their connections in China and other overseas Chinese communities in Southeast Asia, Africa, and Latin America to establish manufacturing facilities. Products manufactured are then imported to the United States. Typically, toys, small tools, electronic appliances, leather goods, and clothing are manufactured in low cost labor areas such as China, Malaysia, Taiwan, and Latin America. Textile plants have been set up in places like the Dominican Republic to bypass textile quotas.

Some new immigrants use their connections in China and other parts of Asia to establish international trading companies. They sell heavy equipment, medical instruments, and local United States products in China, and they purchase consumer goods to sell in the U.S. market. Many grocery stores and restaurants in Chinatown need foodstuffs and products from China; these are supplied by immigrant importers. Some Chinese products like Chinese-style sausages are brought in from Canada, where they are made by the Chinese communities there. Importing sharks' fins and other marine products from Mexico rather than from Asia helps avoid a lot of red tape.

Mr. Gong and His Earth Moving Equipment. Mr. Gong first came to the United States in the 1970s to study business in a large midwestern university. After his graduation, he got a job working in the international division of a multinational corporation. His job was to travel to Asia to do contract negotiations for the company. Mr. Gong speaks English and several major Chinese dialects. Through his business and international travel, he cultivated contacts with other business associates. In 1989, he left his firm to join a heavy equipment manufacturer. His job was to travel to Southeast Asia to sell earth moving equipment to countries investing in infrastructure improvement. In these countries many of the importers are of Chinese descent. Mr. Gong's language abilities in Hakka, Fujianese, and Cantonese were a tremendous help in contract negotiations. Many doors were open to him as a result of his familiarity with the Chinese language, mentality, and modes of social interaction. He soon became an indispensable employee of the company. Since Mr. Gong spends much time in Southeast Asia, his family lives in Singapore. But Mr. Gong also returns to the United States seven or eight times a year for business purposes. In fact, he owns a house in the Bay area. He and his family are able to visit their United States house once a year for two weeks through a special arrangement made with their Chinese tenants. This once a year visit meets residency requirements and affords the Gongs income tax privileges. According to Mr. and Mrs. Gong, by staying in this country for more than thirty days they would lose the advantage of certain tax deductions which are extended to U.S. citizens working overseas. Thus, although the couple lives overseas, they remain connected to the United States and plan to eventually return and settle here permanently.

RETURNING HOME FOR BUSINESS

In the face of recessions, unemployment, and underemployment in the United States in the past ten years, a good many Chinese immigrants have returned to their countries of origin. Others have utilized hometown, friendship, and kinship connections to start joint venture businesses. Still others have offered their expertise to the flourishing economics of their homelands.

After a decade of working in Silicon Valley, Min Wu discovered a secret weapon that he used to start a high-tech venture in Taiwan. This secret weapon was a group of engineers born in Taiwan but trained in Silicon Valley. Using these American-trained engineers, Mr. Wu launched one of the world's largest companies producing programmable memory chips. The sale of his company in 1993 garnered approximately $150 million. Mr. Wu's story is not unique. Increasingly, more and more Taiwanese engineers and other professionals in California are moving back to their homeland to start new businesses, for personal as well as financial reasons. Some have tired of the nagging recessions of the past several years; by contrast, the economy of Taiwan has been growing at 6 percent a year. Further, the living standards in Taiwan are not that much different from those in the United States anymore. In many industrial parks in Taiwan, there are newly constructed tennis courts, swimming pools, and condominiums with bilingual schools specifically for the children of returning engineers (*New York Times,* February 21, 1995).

Some immigrants who have connections with China also look to their homeland for economic opportunities, such as the Kwang brothers. The brothers immigrated to San Francisco in 1993. One planned to start a construction business, the other, an import-export company. Realizing the impossibility of conducting a lucrative business in a recession, they decided to leave the United States. Because of its proximity to China, they settled in Hong Kong with their families. The older brother traveled to China every week to bid on contracts for improvement projects in various newly built hotels. Through his family connections, he has kept busy with a variety of projects since his return in late 1994. The younger brother started a joint venture between the United States and China. He aids a government agency in exporting Chinese porcelain to customers in America and importing agricultural products from the United States. As he has both business knowledge and contacts in the United States and China, he is a perfect conduit for this kind of international trade. In order to keep their residency (both brothers are green card holders), they return to the United States several times a year to visit relatives, including their mother and other siblings living in California. The Kwang brothers are doing well in China, and both have made good use of *guanxi* (connections or networks).

In a rapidly developing economy such as China's, there is the opportunity to do very well financially. One can earn money quickly through trading, construction, and manufacturing, and there is a large consumer base for consumer products. Economic reform in recent years in China has changed Chinese citizens into willing consumers of products from the West, from culinary items to clothing. As China is still a low wage area, many companies look to China to establish manufacturing plants. The growth of industries requires expertise for modern construction projects. Money and talent are both in demand for the development of China's economy.

However, in China there are many bureaucratic procedures that one must follow. For instance, in order to establish a factory, approval from twenty to forty agencies is needed. Complicated procedures often require connections and this opens up the possibilities for corruption. One must have guanxi, or connections, to conduct a business venture in China. The use of guanxi to do business has been a characteristic of both traditional and modern China. Today those immigrants who have a thorough knowledge of the language and culture of China have advantages in developing guanxi.

The Chinese immigrant familiar with both Chinese and American cultures is in an excellent position to conduct international business transactions in China. On the cultural side, such individuals can cultivate their connections with friends, friends of friends, relatives, old classmates and so on. To develop the trust and acceptance needed to make these connections work, immigrants engage in gift giving, attend conventions, go to restaurants, and frequent entertainment facilities such as night clubs, and Karioke clubs. In summation these activities, are known as connection making activities, and are prerequisites for cultivating future business associates. The new Chinese immigrants are creators and manipulators of these spider-web social networks.

There are also Chinese professionals who have been sought by American companies to head business offices in China because of their knowledge of the culture and the language as well as other talents. For instance, the Tandem Corporation in Silicon Valley recently started a software house in Shanghai to train Chinese computer engineers to develop software for Tandem computer systems worldwide. Mr. Spencer Loh, the person chosen to head the office is a Shanghainese-speaking immigrant educated in the United States. Loh has worked for Tandem for many years. He is fluent in English and four Chinese dialects. Since 1993 Tandem's ventures in Shanghai have trained more than 200 Chinese engineers. Although Tandem's U.S. market growth is flat, its Chinese market is growing. Its computers are used to run the Shenzen Stock Exchange systems. Shanghai Tandem also has been developing the ATM switch software for Shanghai's People's Bank of China. It is likely that in the near future more Chinese from the Bay Area will find employment with Shanghai Tandem.

TRANSNATIONAL WORKERS: OTHER COUNTRIES

There are also other global economic connections among the new Chinese immigrants. Some who arrived in San Francisco during the recession in the early 1990s have been forced to seek employment overseas. Through friendship connections, some have been able to get jobs with the companies of their classmates in countries like Nepal and Thailand. Some have gone to Panama to work in their friends' Chinese restaurants. I have also known Chinese immigrants who have gone to work in Chinese garment factories in the Dominican Republic as technicians and supervisors.

A number of Chinese immigrants have come to the United States after having first lived elsewhere in the Chinese diaspora. Mr. Pak first went to Madagascar in the 1970s with the intention of starting a small garment factory. With the help of other Chinese kinsmen who had settled in Madagascar over many generations, Mr. Pak was able to start his business quickly. However, the garment business was not a lucrative one, and he soon sold all of his equipment to local businessmen. Using the money from the sale of his business, Mr. Pak started an import-export business dealing with Chinese products from China. Due to the necessities of his business, he had to travel to many different parts of the world. He came to the United States a while ago and decided to make his home in San Francisco. However, in the past ten years the economy has not been good in California, and Mr. Pak is now back in Madagascar continuing his import and export business. Another new Chinese immigrant works for Mr. Pak, commuting between South Africa, San Francisco and China for the business. Both of these international businessmen have friendship and kinship connections in all three places. Their parents are in China; they have relatives in Africa and they have old classmates in the United States. Their business linkages are thus created and activated in the context of family, kinship, and old school ties.

Mr. Ling was trained as a doctor and his wife as a nurse in China. After they arrived in San Francisco, they found it difficult to practice medicine due to their lack of proper medical degrees.

However, when he was in China, Mr. Ling received some training in acupuncture. Later he continued to take courses and was licensed to practice in Chinatown. As it turns out, this business is quite competitive: there are many Chinese acupuncturists in the Chinatown community. Through the help of old friends from China, Mr. Ling was able to get a visa to go to Cuba which, in the past, had a sizable Chinese population. Today Mr. Ling and his wife are doing very well in Cuba and try to reciprocate the assistance of friends by inviting them for visits to Cuba.

The diasporic Chinese communities around the world have become a resource for the Chinese immigrants in San Francisco. Through family, kinship, friendship, and hometown connections, classmates or other personal links, a Chinese immigrant can always find an economic opportunity overseas. In the past several years, there have been discussions among the overseas Chinese about developing a more formal structure to organize Chinese businessmen around the world. There have even been conventions for this purpose. One such convention will be held in Tokyo next year solely on the topic of the possibilities of coordinating business networks among overseas Chinese businessmen. Thus, overseas Chinese communities around the world are recognized as resources, both formally and informally, among the Chinese immigrants. Networking activities can be seen as a collective response to the globalization process of the world's economy.

One immigrant told me that he left China after the Tiananmen incident in June, 1989. He came to this country but had a difficult time finding employment. However, using his family connections in China and South Africa, he was able to get a contract to assemble auto parts in Johannesburg, where the infrastructure was more suitable for certain industrial activities. He was able to ship materials from China and have them assembled in Johannesburg. The assembled sections were then transported back to China. He has used his guanxi in China and Africa and has been doing a brisk business as the middleman.

In Silicon Valley some Chinese engineers return to places like Singapore and Malaysia to work in high-tech industries. In fact, the Singapore government, hoping to become a technological powerhouse in Asia, has made deliberate efforts to attract talented Chinese to their country.

Of all the transnational migrant workers I interviewed, I saw no evidence of an abandonment of their residency or citizenship in the United States. For the Chinese immigrants transnational-ism is an economic adaptive strategy in a changing world (cf. Basch, Schiller, and Blanc 1994). Because many new immigrants have made commitments to the United States, overseas employ-ment often reflects only a temporary adaptive strategy.

CONCLUSION

Realizing that the world has gradually developed into a single production system, many wealthy businessmen and educated professionals want to become players in the global economy. To do so, they are not hesitant to use family, kinship, and friendship connections to organize business firms, find employment and to invest and expand their business activities. Some have successful-ly built international social networks to adjust to the changing economy of the world. Among these new Chinese immigrants, one sees dynamism and ingenuity—they are truly global migrants and shapers of their own destinies.

Even immigrants who are not particularly wealthy or educat-ed have sometimes benefited from returning to Asia to establish lucrative businesses, participate in economic joint ventures, or launch special business projects. These transnationals have to leave their families in the Bay Area and make personal sacrifices in order to make a living for themselves. The global production system has a way of relocating people and at the same time open-ing new spheres of economic activities for Chinese immigrants who have few other comparable opportunities in the United States, especially during periods of unemployment and recession.

Thinking and acting globally have become trademarks of many new Chinese immigrants. To what extent this trend will continue remains an exciting topic for future researchers and scholars of the overseas Chinese.

Survival and Adaptation in Modern America

Immigrants not only adapt to fit into the American social landscape, they also at the very same time bring about changes in their new home. The presence of new Chinese immigrants in San Francisco has had a ripple effect on the established ethnic community, the city, and the larger society. And, as they come to terms with life in San Francisco, the Chinese immigrants often begin to see themselves in new ways and devise new strategies for coping with the American context.

CONTRIBUTIONS OF THE NEW CHINESE IMMIGRANTS

The new immigrants have changed the boundaries of many neighborhoods. As mentioned earlier, they have settled in areas such as Chinatown, the Richmond and Sunset Districts, Hillsborough, as well as less fashionable neighborhoods like Visitation Valley and Ingleside. Places that were not popular before have been made more desirable by the presence of immigrant families. The new Chinese immigrants have renovated old houses, making neighborhoods more attractive and increasing property values. Many commercial areas of the city have also changed with the influx of new Chinese immigrants. The Mission District is an example with new housing as well as many Chinese restaurants and garment factories.

In fact, the new Hong Kong immigrants, together with those from Taiwan and mainland China, have made San Francisco the third largest garment manufacturing center in the United States, trailing only New York City and Los Angeles. Many estimates place the value of the annual garment business in San Francisco at seven to eight billion dollars (*San Francisco Chronicle*, September 14, 1993). Immigrant workers, paid low wages, help provide the mostly white manufacturers with large profits, and they support many of the retail apparel stores throughout the Bay Area.

Chinese immigrants are also prominent in the real estate business. In 1990 one in four homes sold in San Francisco was purchased by a Chinese person (Wong 1994). The wave of home purchases support both Chinese and non-Chinese real estate agents, brokers, mortgage companies, and banking institutions in the Bay Area. Additionally, many of the large office buildings in downtown San Francisco are owned and have been renovated by Hong Kong immigrants. Improvement projects in the high-rise office buildings have benefited the construction trade in San Francisco. Because of the strong interest among Chinese in buying property, many wealthy Chinese immigrants have gone into the real estate business, with both individual and, more importantly, corporate purchases for speculation. In the 1960s there were only seventy real estate companies in San Francisco, but this number has mushroomed since then. In addition, mortgage companies and title companies run by Chinese have been established to facilitate real estate transactions among recent immigrants.

Contrary to the popular perception that immigrants drain the economy and the welfare systems of the United States, Chinese immigrants have created employment opportunities not only for other Chinese, but for non-Chinese as well. In ethnic businesses, such as restaurants, grocery stores, and garment factories, there are non-Chinese employees. Immigrant entrepreneurs in Silicon Valley employ many Chinese and non-Chinese professionals. In 1983 Hong Kong immigrant Steve Hui established Everex, a high-tech company which employs many white technicians and engineers. Similarly, computer companies such as Sun Microsystems, Spectrum Semiconductor Manufacturers, ACR Systems and Systender International Corporation all hire many white employees. Many immigrant banks such as the United Savings Bank, the American Asian Bank, the Bank of Orient, the Trans National Bank, and the National American Bank also employ non-Chinese.

In the hotel business, too, the new Chinese immigrants operate a number of first-class international hotels, such as Parc 55, the Meridien Hotel, Holiday Inn Crown Plaza in Burlingame and the Hyatt Regency in Oakland. All of these establishments employ non-Chinese workers. Unlike the Chinese immigrants in the old days, the new immigrants are able to participate more fully in the marketplace as employers and thus contribute to the mainstream economy. The Chinese immigrants also help generate profits for American companies with their talents and special training. For instance, Mr. Kai-Fu Lee, an immigrant engineer, guided the development of the Chinese dictation system for Apple Computer Inc. With this software program, a Chinese speaker can input Chinese characters into a computer. Many experts believe that the new Macintosh program will become popular in Taiwan, China, Singapore and other places where Chinese speakers predominate. The product was introduced in Beijing in October, 1995 and was named the best overall product from America (*San Francisco Examiner*, January 8, 1996).

The influx of immigrants from Taiwan, Hong Kong, and China has fostered curiosity about East Asia. Many San Franciscans, through contact with the new immigrants, have developed a special interest in Asia. International travel between the Pacific Rim countries and San Francisco is the most lucrative route for several major airlines. Realizing the importance of connections with Asia, San Francisco Mayor Frank Jordan led a trade mission to Hong Kong and Shanghai in 1993. His predecessor, Mayor Art Agnos, also made similar trips. Shanghai is a sister city of San Francisco and Mayor Jordan had also hoped to develop a sister-city relationship with Hong Kong. A spokesman from the former mayor's office once hinted that San Francisco could learn from Hong Kong's experience in becoming a center of banking, finance and international trade. The Chinese immigrants are also significant in the export-import sector and in international transportation. With a knowledge of the Chinese language and culture, they are important facilitators of international trade and international shipping with Hong Kong, China, Taiwan, Singapore and other countries.

Bay Area residents may benefit in more direct ways from the presence of Chinese immigrants. Chinese engineers, architects, roofers, gardeners, brake repairers, movers, construction workers, and auto mechanics often provide less expensive services than non-Chinese businesses—a plus for consumers. Many of the immigrants from Asia are fashion conscious and thus customers of boutiques, buying designer clothing and other consumer products. San Francisco marketers have been trying to reach these

Asian immigrant consumers. On August 21, 1989 the *San Francisco Examiner* reported that many advertisers in the *Asian Yellow Pages* were non-Asian. Executives at several marketing research companies whom I interviewed told me that many white establishments are trying to capture Chinese immigrant consumers. American immigration lawyers, telephone companies, and banking institutions often appeal to Chinese customers for their patronage. They run prominent ads just to target Chinese immigrants. Thus Chinese immigrants constitute an important consumer base for the mainstream economy.

Inevitably, conflicts develop between immigrants and established residents. In the wake of neighborhood changes and increased housing prices mentioned earlier, resentment of the newcomers does develop. Problems with street gangs and the expense of bilingual education programs are additional social costs that the immigrants and the American society share. However, taxes paid by the immigrants and other contributions they make to the economy, American culture and the social system outweigh the social costs incurred. The Chinese, like the pioneer immigrants in the early days, have enriched America. From science to literature, education to technology, labor to management, talented Chinese immigrants have made important contributions.

And yet, all of this is not to imply that discrimination against the Chinese immigrant community no longer exists. There are still many hurdles for Chinese in America to overcome. Many Chinese immigrants believe that they are purposefully excluded from administrative jobs in city and state governments—and an organization called Chinese for Affirmative Action has substantiated this claim (Wong 1994). Some professionals complain about the glass ceiling blocking career promotions and advancement. The glass ceiling is one of the reasons why some Chinese immigrants return to their homeland to work, or leave their present companies to start their own firms. Some workers in factories and business firms complain that they are paid less than whites with similar education and skills. An article in *Newsweek* (May 11, 1987) called this phenomenon "topping out." Although Chinese continue to be hired at entry levels, they are often find it difficult to be promoted to the higher echelons. Dr. Chia-Wei Woo had this to say about the lack of top level administrators at San Francisco State University (which has 35 percent Asian students):

Isn't it weird that I'm the only Chinese university president? It's ludicrous.... There are 15–25 percent in the faculty, but only 2 percent in administration. And we're not screaming? (Yu 1987, 121)

An engineer and investor, David Lee, from Silicon Valley, made a similar statement concerning employment biases against the Chinese in the business community:

I have invested in many companies. Few people are willing to support Chinese. I always want Chinese in the companies. A lot of companies don't want to promote Chinese—they just want to use them. It's so easy for people to say "you have a communication problem." Sometimes it may be true, but sometimes it's an excuse, and the person has real ability. (Yu 1987, 86)

Discrimination and prejudice persist at the neighborhood level. Some whites do not welcome Chinese home buyers; a common fear is that the Chinese will demolish the houses to build larger ones or to construct apartment blocks. While white neighbors are arguing on the basis of community character, the Chinese experience these complaints as racism. Some Chinese desire larger homes to accommodate their families, which tend to be bigger than those of white Americans.

The new immigrants are optimistic that these discriminatory practices will diminish in time. Meanwhile, they have learned how to complain and how to use the media and human rights agencies to seek redress. They also have learned that they need to participate in the electoral process to elect politicians who are sympathetic to Chinese and immigrant issues. Thus the stereotype of the Chinese as passive does not apply to the Chinese immigrants as a group.

POLITICS AND THE NEW IMMIGRANTS

Unlike the earlier settlers, the new immigrants have a keen awareness of international and domestic politics and economic developments. The new immigrants are particularly sensitive to world events. Living in Hong Kong, Taiwan and China, many Chinese have learned that the international financial market, as well as political changes in the rest of the world, especially in the

United Kingdom and the United States, can affect their well-being. After immigrating to the United States, they continue to keep this international mind-set. They continue to read newspapers from Hong Kong, China, and Taiwan. There are at least eight Chinese language daily newspapers circulating in San Francisco. One newspaper *Singtao* has an English supplement with news specifically targeted to young Hong Kong Chinese who have difficulty reading Chinese characters. Apart from local and American news, the contents of *Singtao* are transmitted daily from Hong Kong via satellite. The news is reported and analyzed from the point of view of Hong Kong. To balance this, many new immigrants also read the *World Journal*, a pro-Taiwan publication. Many new immigrants read the two newspapers to gain a more complete coverage and two points of view. Additionally, there are daily newspapers from China available around the Bay Area. In a sense, the Chinese immigrants stay in tune with the world through information from the Chinese media, supplemented by information from the American media.

Domestically, the new immigrants are aware of the importance of political power. Unlike the old immigrants, most of the new arrivals want to become naturalized citizens of the United States as soon as possible. Many are interested in participating in American public affairs. New immigrants are sensitive to social injustices against Chinese Americans. Unlike their forebears, the new immigrants have learned to fight individually and collectively. Among the new immigrants, there are Chinese running for political office at the national, state and city levels. New, educated immigrants have run for various political offices such as judgeships, school board seats, and city council positions. Successful examples in San Francisco include Julie Teng, Mabel Teng, Lily Sing and Tom Hsieh. In 1988–1989, former Mayor Art Agnos appointed twenty Chinese Americans (mostly immigrants) to serve on city commissions. Additionally, the new immigrants support both Chinese and non-Chinese candidates who serve the interests of the Chinese community. The Chinese in San Francisco are overwhelmingly supportive of the recent appointments of Fred Lau as the new police chief, Doug Wong as a police commissioner, Wayne Hu as a member of the Board of Permit Appeals, and Lonnie Chin as a commissioner on the Library Commission.

The new immigrants have also learned to use ethnicity to form interest groups for social action. An example is the Organization of Chinese Americans (OCA) that was established to lobby the United States Congress and the White House on behalf of the Chinese. In 1983, the OCA urged a Senate subcommittee to lift restrictive immigration quotas for colonies. More recently, the OCA succeeded in persuading the United States Postal Commission to issue a stamp to recognize the contributions of the Chinese in America. The OCA has many Hong Kong and Taiwanese new immigrants as members and even has a chapter in Hong Kong to serve the Chinese Americans there. Other organizations and interest groups include Mr. Frank Wong's Foundation for Chinese Democracy, the Alliance of Hong Kong Chinese in America, Asian Immigrant Women Advocates, the Asian Law Caucus and the Chinese American Citizens Alliance. All these serve the ethnic interests of the Chinese in the Bay Area.

The new immigrants in San Francisco realize that they need to participate in politics to improve their lives. Favorable legislation, political appointments, and interest group influence can be used to fight discrimination, to work toward the American Dream and to establish the Chinese in the San Francisco Bay Area.

ESTABLISHING ROOTS AND IDENTITIES IN AMERICA

Among the new immigrants, establishing roots—*Lo Di Sang Gen*—is now the professed ideology. Immigrant churches are one place where this ideology is stressed. In the Bay Area there is a proliferation of Chinese Christian churches. Hong Kong immigrants usually prefer to go to churches with priests, ministers or pastors from Hong Kong who speak Cantonese while immigrants from Taiwan go to churches with services in Mandarin. My research data indicate that immigrant clergy from Hong Kong and Taiwan tend to emphasize active participation in American life. These churches contrast markedly with those serving the local-born Chinese and immigrants from mainland China, which tend to emphasize spiritual salvation and evangelical fundamentalism.

Contrary to the old immigrants, the new arrivals do not plan to return to their homeland for permanent resettlement. For the old immigrants, their ideology was *Lo Yeh Gui Gen*—returning to their original roots after they have established themselves economically. This was a sojourning ideology, i.e., to make a fortune overseas and then return to the old country. For the new immigrants, the mindset is to establish oneself and to settle permanently in the host country. However, this does not indicate a total surrender of one's ethnicity. After interviewing many informants in the past several years, I have discovered that the question of ethnic identification and behavior for the new Chinese immigrants is a complex one. Many factors are involved in shaping ethnic identity and behavior, including which country they departed from and under what circumstances. There are at least four dominant types of ethnic adaptation among the new Chinese immigrants: (1) complete assimilation to the host culture, or "Westernization;" (2) a hybrid ethnicity, combining Chinese humanism with American pragmatism, technology and democracy; (3) retaining Chinese culture and maintaining Chinese identity in the United States and (4) socializing and getting along with Chinese people overseas but remaining detached from Asia and concerns with ethnic identity.

Complete Assimilation

Before emigrating some Chinese immigrants view the United States positively and aspire to become American. They watch American movies, learn American English and listen to American music. After their arrival in the United States, they prefer not to socialize with other Chinese and to work toward complete immersion in American culture. They make efforts to avoid other Chinese, and they prefer to work with and live among white people. Some Chinese immigrants feel ready to completely turn away from Chinese culture. This group of people is a small minority and is composed of relatively young immigrants. One couple told me the following: "Why emigrate to the United States if we want to keep Chinese customs? If you want to be American you cannot be Chinese. What kind of country is this? If you are in Rome, you behave like a Roman. When you enter a village, you follow the custom of the villagers."

This is the argument of some westernized Chinese immigrants. Mr. Lu of Hong Kong, one informant, told me that even when he was in Hong Kong, he did not act like other Chinese. During the lunch break every day, he went to a music store to purchase compact discs of western classical music. He enjoyed his outings to the music store every day. His sister is now in America and is married to a Korean who has the same commitment to American culture. Mr. Lu was educated in Hong Kong and England and he said that when he emigrated from Hong Kong he left his culture behind. He wants to marry an American white woman and he eats only American food. He prefers not to socialize with other Chinese.

Westernized Chinese, like Mr. Lu, are not only found in America. In Hong Kong, some students who were educated in Great Britain at Eton, Oxford, or Cambridge often idealized foreign culture and preferred to work and interact with people from England when they returned home. Westernization has been a topic of long-standing public debate in China since the May Fourth Movement of 1919. One famous scholar by the name of Hu Shi argued that the Chinese should discard all their customs and westernize themselves. He was a graduate of Columbia University and once said that the "moon is even rounder in America."

Hybrid Ethnicity

Another group—the majority—of new immigrants want to have the best of both worlds by combining Chinese and American cultural traits. They would like to be both Chinese and American at the same time. They feel comfortable with the Chinese way of human interaction: the emphasis on smooth and harmonious social relations, the concern with *renqin* (human feeling) and human collectivity and a consideration for the aged. On the other hand, they also admire the pragmatism of American culture. They like American technology, democracy, and sexual equality. A popular saying is *Zhung Xie Wei Ti, Zi Xue Wei Yung*—Chinese learning in substance and Western learning in practice. People in this group told me that they enjoy living in America but are not yet ready to give up the Chinese way of interacting with each other, with the family and with other Chinese. They told me that there is a certain warmth in the Chinese way of social interaction that they prefer to white Americans' frankness and impersonal interaction patterns. As a result, these individuals long to synthesize the American and the Chinese ways of living into a hybrid of Chinese and American traits. Here is what one informant had to say: "I could never get used to the American way of dealing with people. Look at them. They change their spouse as often as they change their cars. When their parents are old, they are on their own. Children live far away from them and do not take care of them. Look at the way they treat their employees. If the employees perform well, they are kept. If they do not perform according to expectation, they are just fired coolly. There is no *renqin*. On the other hand, the American way of rule of law is good. One person one vote and everyone should be responsible for his or her actions is something I like. Everyone is equal in front of the law is good. I like democracy."

My female informants, too, would like to have a synthesis between the east and the west, between the Chinese and the American. They told me that it is convenient to be a housewife in America. The high-tech kitchen, the fast food restaurants and other modern conveniences give them much freedom. Some of those who work feel that they are treated better in the workplaces here than in their countries of origin. Yet all of my female informants felt that there is too much violence against women in America, which they attributed to the unbridled individualism of Americans. And the Chinese women I spoke to also complained about impersonality in American culture and the lack of *renqin* (human feeling) in human interaction.

To Be an Authentic Chinese in America

Some Chinese immigrants keep their Chinese cultural orientation in dealing with things, people, and the unknown. They celebrate all the customs and festivals of Chinese culture. In their homes, they use only Chinese style furniture and, following the advice of the geomancers (*Feng Shui* experts), eat only Chinese food. They work only with Chinese firms and interact only with Chinese people. Many of them do not speak any English and deal only with Chinese people in America. This group includes many immigrants from the rural areas of mainland China and some uneducated Chinese from Hong Kong. They most closely resemble the early immigrants from traditional China in their outlook. They feel that there is nothing worthwhile for them to learn from America; this is only a country for them to make a living and to establish their economic foundation. Some of them frequent Chinese temples, traditional associations in Chinatown, and socialize with each other. They watch only Chinese TV programs and videos, and play mahjong with their Chinese friends. When they work, they work in Chinese establishments such as grocery stores, restaurants or garment factories. They are very isolated from the larger society and often times fear America. One informant complained to me that in America even the streets and parks are not constructed with people in mind. He said that when it rains people in the streets just get wet, and the parks have too few chairs or places with cover. Another informant complained that America is good for the young but ignores the old. He said: "When you are old you cannot get a job anywhere in America!"

Detached and Uninterested in Questions of Identity

This group of Chinese immigrants includes jump-ship sailors, exiled students, and itinerant businessmen. It should be noted that people who do not come to this country legally are not respected in the Chinese community. They are given menial jobs and paid very low wages. Students who left China after the Tiananmen incident in June 4, 1989 may be granted asylum in the United States, but many are unsettled emotionally. They are often uninterested in the question of ethnic identity in America. Some itinerant businessmen who travel continuously from America to China or other places also have no interest in thinking about the issue of identity. One informant told me: "I have no time to think about identity because I have to make a living. It is a waste of time to talk about this useless thing!"

Making a living and the routine of day-to-day existence occupies much of the time of people in this group. I met one exiled student who has four jobs to keep him afloat in America. He teaches martial arts in the morning in a park in San Francisco, goes to school in the afternoons, and works in a Chinese restaurant in the evenings. During the weekends, he had kung fu classes. Another exiled student told me that he had a hard time getting a job in Chinatown because he does not speak Cantonese. He had to go to Japantown to get a job in a Korean restaurant. For him the question of identity is meaningless. He said although he is a Chinese person, he could not get a job from a Chinese establishment. He still thinks about his friends who died in China during the Tiananmen Incident. Some of these exiled students feel comfortable talking with each other about their common interests and common problems. For this group of people, whether they are itinerant businessmen, jump-ship sailors or exiled students, they prefer to invest their energy elsewhere than to think about their identity.

CONCLUSIONS: ECONOMIC ADAPTATION AND ETHNICITY

The Chinese immigrants in the San Francisco Bay Area have utilized their cultural as well as economic resources to meet the economic challenges of the region. In the past the labor of the Chinese immigrants was needed for mining, railroad building, and agriculture. After 1884 these immigrants started to move away from rural areas to cities, finding work in the ethnic niche. The creation of ethnic businesses was an ingenious way for the early immigrants to avoid direct confrontation with white laborers in the market place. These Chinese ethnic enterprises were labor-intensive, nonconfrontational and noncompetitive with white business and labor.

The Chinese immigrants who moved into cities concentrated themselves residentially into certain neighborhoods where traditional Chinese social structure and organization was established to protect their ethnic community and businesses. These areas became known as the Chinatowns of the United States. They were both a monument to racism and an adaptive device for survival used by the immigrants. These old immigrants functioned within the context of the traditional social structure, and emphasized their ethnic identity. Their ethnic enclave was not only how they made a living, it was also a cultural frontier. The various associations, built on traditional principles of social organization in rural China, were important in many immigrant activities, such as credit formation, business partnership, conflict resolution and socialization. The old immigrants were proud to be real Chinese and believed that the United States was only a temporary location to accumulate wealth and fortune. After they reached this goal, they planned to return to their ancestral land, begin an entrepreneurial endeavor or retire elegantly. They sympathized with China and were supportive of many of the social and political events in China, especially in the republican course of overthrowing the Manchu dynasty. They were the patriotic overseas Chinese who vowed to one day save China. They were not hesitant to use their image of real Chinese to compete for political leadership within the Chinese community. Some were even invited back to the motherland to be decorated as *chaio lin* (or *kiu ling* in Cantonese—meaning leaders of the overseas Chinese) by the Kuomintang government. In fact, Dr. Sun Yat-sen called the overseas Chinese the Mothers of the Chinese Revolution. Thus politically, economically, and socially, it was seen to be advantageous to embrace a Chinese identity, especially in the face of exclusion and discrimination such as the old immigrants experienced.

After 1965 the new Chinese immigrants who came to California have included many professionals as well as a small number of very wealthy individuals. Many arrive with their families and this infusion has completely changed the bachelor community of old. Now immigrants come to establish roots in America. Families have turned out to be important resources for the new immigrants. Indeed, family firms have characterized much of new Chinese immigrant entrepreneurship. At the same time, the traditional associations which served the old immigrants have declined in importance.

In both enclave and nonenclave businesses, Chinese immigrant businessmen use their families, traditional social etiquette, and Chinese culture to pursue their economic goals. While they treasure Chinese humanism, they also rely on American pragmatism, and they use both to achieve their goal of settling permanently in America. Most embrace a hybrid identity combining Chinese and American traits. However, they also hope that the future generation will be totally accepted by American society.

The children of the new immigrants, just like many American born Chinese, hope for unreserved acceptance by the host society: they want to be integrated into the mainstream American culture, and economy. First generation immigrants, through their ethnic enterprises, help their children receive college educations to further their chances of achieving the American Dream. Because of this drive to be accepted by mainstream society and to be part of the larger culture many second generation individuals now emphasize integration. Some even go to the extreme of renouncing their cultural heritage. However, America is now experimenting with the concept of multiculturalism, which emphasizes the contributions of many cultures. Many children of the immigrants have also gradually returned to their roots. Instead of totally abandoning their traditional culture, they are taking courses in ethnic studies and other cultural disciplines. They hope that in addition to their specialized training, education in ethnic and cultural studies may enhance their employment opportunities. Looking for roots now has its own reward.

Ethnic culture and traditions can be viewed as an asset in American life. Among the new Chinese immigrants, ethnic resources such as family, kinship ties, values, language, and connections have helped them adjust to America and to the rest of the world. From enclave businesses to international businesses, and from Chinatown to China, traditional values and the old fabric of kinship and friendship ties have assisted the entrepreneurial pursuits of the Chinese immigrants.

At the same time, Chinese immigrants have been eager to acquire United States citizenship and to participate in the American Dream. Chinese ethnocentrism certainly exists, but no more than the ethnocentrism of other ethnic groups in America. The idea that the Chinese community is a model community, which is self-sufficient and does not require assistance from the larger society, has been shown to be a myth. Indeed, the Chinese community in San Francisco has never been a self-sufficient community or without internal conflicts. Its economic well-being is at the mercy of the larger society. Macroenvironmental circumstances have compelled the Chinese to pursue certain lines of business, develop particular social structures, and foster social networks to make a living.

There are historical, legal, social, and economic factors that affect the participation of the Chinese in mainstream American life. Most notable among these were the discriminatory policies enacted in the 1800's, (discussed in Chapter 2). From 1882 until 1965, Chinese immigrants were considered unwelcome people in the United States (Miller 1969). The economic activities of the Chinese have been undertaken within the constraints of U.S. society. Restricted economic opportunity induced the Chinese to use economic adaptive strategies, such as the formation of ethnic niches like Chinatowns, or to engage in noncompetitive businesses such as hand laundries and grocery stores. With the changing attitudes toward ethnic groups and civil rights legislation of the 1960s, opportunities for residential, economic, and social mobility among the Chinese improved. Historical legal and economic discrimination against the Chinese generated the defensive response of the Chinese. Some wanted to return to their roots, others wanted to get rid of their cultural baggage and assimilate into American society. Recent legal protections and more open economic opportunities have precipitated wider participation and larger contributions of ethnic Chinese in contemporary America. A vast majority of the Chinese immigrants now hope to establish roots in America.

The transformation of the global economy, the recession in America in the past several years, and the glass ceiling have contributed to changes among the new immigrants. Some have become transnational workers and some return to China, Taiwan or Hong Kong. Yet the overwhelming majority of the Chinese want to keep their American passports and residency and settle in this country permanently. The ethnic businesses in and out of Chinatown, professional careers in Silicon Valley, and transnational business activities are adaptive strategies and responses to the macroeconomic or global economic environments.

The ethnic identities and economic activities of the Chinese cannot be understood in isolation from the larger society. However, knowledge of conditions in the larger society cannot alone predict the actions of the Chinese. Hence, investigations of ethnic identities and economic adaptations in an immigrant community must take into account socioeconomic conditions and restraints of the macro context as well as social and cultural factors within the immigrant community itself.

References and Suggested Readings

Amyot, Jacques
  1973. The Manila Chinese. Quezon City: Institute of Philippine Culture.

Asian Week
  1991. Asians in America: 1990 Census.

Barth, Fredrik
  1966. Models of Social Organization. Royal Anthropological Institute Occasional Paper. No. 23. Glasgow: University Press.

Basch, Linda, Nina Glick Schiller and Christina Szanton Blanc
  1994. Nations Unbound: Transnational Projects, Postcolonial Predicaments and Deterritorialized Nation-States. Amsterdam: Gordon and Breach Publishers.

Benedict, Burton
  1968. "Family Firms and Economic Development." Southwestern Journal of Anthropology 24(1):1–19.

———.
  1979. "Family Firms and Firm Families." In Sidney Greenfield, Arnold Strickon and Robert T. Aubey, Eds. Entrepreneurs in Cultural Context. Albuquerque: University of New Mexico Press.

Chan, J. B. L. and Y. W. Cheung
  1985. "Ethnic Resources and Business Enterprise: A Study of Chinese Business in Tornonto." Human Organization 44(2):142–154.

Chan, Kwok Bun and Claire Chiang
  1994. Stepping Out. Singapore: Prentice-Hall.

Chau, T. T.
  1991. "Approaches to Succession in East Asian Business Organization." Family Business Review 4(2):161–179.

Chin, Thomas, Him Mark Lai and Philipe Choy
  1975. A History of the Chinese in California: A Syllabus. San Francisco: Chinese Historical Society of America.

Coser, L.
1974. Greedy Institutions. New York: Free Press.

Davis, William H.
1929. Seventy-Five Years in California. San Francisco: J. Howell.

De Guignes, Joseph
1761. Reserches Sur Les Navigations des Chinois du Cote de L'Amerique. Paris: Academie des Inscriptions.

Donckels, Rik and Eberhard Frohlich
1991. "Are Family Businesses REAL Different? Europeans Experiences from STRATOS." Family Business Review 4(2):149–160.

Fang, Zhongpu
1980. "Did Chinese Buddhist Reach America 1,000 Years Before Columbus?" China Reconstructs (August):65.

Fishman, Joshua
1966. Language Loyalty in the United States. The Hague: Mouton.

Fong, Timothy P.
1994. The First Suburban Chinatown. Philadelphia: Temple University Press.

Gordon, Milton
1964. Assimilation in American Life. New York: Oxford University Press.

Greenfield, Sidney, Arnold Strickon and Robert T. Aubey
1979. Entrepreneurs in Cultural Context. Alburquerque: University of New Mexico Press.

Him Mark Lai
1992. From Chinese Overseas Chinese to Ethnic Chinese (in Chinese). Hong Kong: Joint Publishing.

Hoy, William
1942. The Chinese Six Companies. San Francisco: Chinese Consolidated Benevolent Association.

Hsu, P. S. C.
1984. "The Influence of Family Structure and Values on Business Organizations in Oriental Cultures: A Comparison of China and Japan." Proceedings of the Academy of International Business.

Hsu, Francis L. K.
1981. American and Chinese: Passage of Difference. Honolulu: University Press of Hawaii.

Kearney, Michael
1991. Borders and Boundaries of the State and Self at the End of the Empire. Journal of Historical Sociology 4(1):52–74.

Kwang, Yu
1987. Stories of the Gold Mountain (in Chinese). Hong Kong: Dai Ka Publishers.

Lee, Rose Hum
1947. The Chinese Communities in the Rocky Mountain Region." Unpublished Ph.D. Dissertation. Chicago: University of Chicago.

———.
1960. The Chinese in the United States of America. Hong Kong: Hong Kong University Press.

———.
1979[1947] The Growth and Decline of Chinese Communities in the Rocky Mountain Region. New York: Arno Press and the New York Times.

Light, Ivan
1972. Ethnic Enterprises in America. Berkeley: University of California Press.

———.
1984. "Immigrant and Ethnic Enterprise in North America." Ethnic and Racial Studies 7(2):195–216.

Loo, Chalsa M.
1991. Chinatown: Most Time, Hard Time. New York: Praeger.

Mangiafico, Luciano
1988. Contemporary American Immigrants. New York: Praeger.

McClain, Charles J.
1994. In Search of Equality: The Chinese Struggle against Discrimination in Nineteenth-Century America. Berkeley: University of California Press.

Miller, Stuart Creighton
1969. The Unwelcome Immigrant. Berkeley: University of California Press.

New York Times
February 21, 1995. "Skilled Asians Leaving U.S. for High-Tech Jobs at Home."

Newsweek
May 11, 1987. "Topping Out."

Park, R. E.
  1950. Race and Culture. Glencoe: The Free Press.

Piore, Michael J.
  1986. "The Shifting Grounds for Immigration." Annals of the American Academy of Sciences 485:23–33.

Portes, Alejandro
  1980. "Immigrant Earnings: Cuban and Mexican Immigrants in the United States." International Migration Review 14(3):315–341.

Portes, Alejandro and Ruben Rumbaut
  1990. Immigrant America, A Portrait. Berkeley: University of California Press.

Rosaldo, Renato
  1993. Borderlands of Race and Inequality. Paper delivered at the Spring Meetings of Society for Cultural Anthropology. Washington D.C.

San Francisco Examiner
  April 20, 1989. "A New Money Elite."
  August 21, 1989. "Asia Influence Comes of Age."
  April 19, 1994. "Immigrants Make More than Natives in the Professions."
  July 7, 1994. "East Bay Astronaut Fulfilling Lifelong Dream."
  September 17, 1994. "Silicon Valley Software Firm Sails into Shanghai."
  March 16, 1995. "Fear, Bias Build 'ceiling'."
  January 8, 1996. "Mac Mandarin."

San Francisco Chronicle
  April 29, 1993. "American Dream Sours in N.Y."
  May, 19, 1996. "Yes, I Am A Traitor."
  September 14, 1993. "A Plan to End 'Sweatshops'."

San Jose Mercury News
  November 22, 1992. "Minorities are Majority in 137 Occupations in County."
  May 30, 1993. "Newcomers Don't Strain the Job Market."
  August 22, 1993. "Tide of Opportunities Turns for Taiwanese Engineers."

Sandmeyer, E. E.
  1973. The Anti-Chinese Movement in California. Urbana: The University of Illinois Press.

Sassen-Koob, Saskia
  1988. The Mobility of Labor and Capital: A Study in International Investment and Labor Flow. New York: Cambridge University Press.

Skeldon, Ronald
1994. Reluctant Exiles? Armonk, New York: M. E. Sharpe.

Steiner, Stan
1979. Fusang: The Chinese Who Built America. New York: Harper and Row Publishers.

Tien, Ju-kang
1953. The Chinese in Sarawak. London: London School of Economics and Political Science.

Time
November 21, 1994. "Tigers in the Lab."

U.S. Census of Population, 1990.

Waldinger, Roger
1986. Through the Eye of the Needle: Immigrants and Enterprise in New York's Garment Trades. New York: New York University Press.

_____.
1989. "Structural Opportunity of Economic Advantage? Immigrant Business Development in New York." International Migration Review 23(1):48–72.

Waldinger, Roger, Howard Aldrich and Robin Ward
1990. Ethnic Entrepreneurs. Newbury Park: Sage Publications.

Wallerstein, Emmanuel
1974. The Modern World System. New York: Acadmic Press.

_____.
1979. The Capitalist World Economy. Cambridge, MA: Cambridge University Press.

Wilson, Kenneth L. and Alejandro Portes
1980. "Immigrant Enclaves: An Analysis of the Labor Market Experiences of Cubans in Miami." American Journal of Sociology 86(2):295–319.

Wong, Bernard P.
1979. A Chinese American Community: Ethnicity and Survival Strategies. Singapore: Chopmen Enterprises.

_____.
1982. Chinatown: Economic Adaptation and Ethnic Identity of the Chinese. New York: Holt, Rinehart and Winston.

_____.
1987a. "The Role of Ethnicity in Enclave Enterprises: A Study of the Chinese Garment Factories in New York City." Human Organization 46(2):120–130.

_____.
1987b. "The Chinese: New Immigrants in New York's Chinatown." In Nancy Foner, Ed., New Immigrants in New York. New York: Columbia University Press.

_____.
1988. Patronage, Brokerage, Entrepreneurship and the Chinese Community of New York. New York: AMS Press.

_____.
1994. "Hong Kong Immigrants in San Francisco." In Ronald Skeldon, Ed., New York: M. E. Sharpe.

Wong, Bernard, Becky McReynolds and Wynnie Wong
1992. "Chinese Family Firms in the San Francisco Bay Area." Family Business Review 5(4):355–372.

Wong, S. L.
1985. "The Chinese Family Firm: A Model." British Journal of Sociology 36(1):58–72.

Wu, Cheng-Tsu
1958. Chinese People and Chinatown in New York City. Ph.D. Thesis. Ann Arbor: University Microfilms.

Yu, Connie Young
1987. Profiles in Excellence. Stanford: Stanford Area Chinese Club.

Zhou, Min
1992. Chinatown: The Socioeconomic Potential of an Urban Enclave. Philadelphia: Temple University Press.